"This book is really an eye-opener. If you care ... Turner's book is a must-read. He clearly lays out an alarming Roberts Court pattern to abuse the First Amendment to achieve a conservative outcome."

—Barbara Boxer, former US Senator and co-host of *The Boxer Podcast*

"Justice Elena Kagan wrote of the conservatives weaponizing the First Amendment. Bill Turner tells us what this means and why it ultimately is about empowering corporations and the religious right. In a very clear, accessible book, he has sounded an alarm that we must heed."

—Erwin Chemerinsky, Dean and Jesse H. Choper Distinguished Professor of Law, University of California, Berkeley School of Law

"In this excellent and timely book, William Bennett Turner shows us how our current Supreme Court has, case by case, reshaped First Amendment protection for free speech, to the benefit of corporations, special interests, and conservative causes. *Free Speech for Some* is lucid, judicious, and brimming with authoritative insights into this troubling development."

—Thelton E. Henderson, former Chief Judge, United States District Court

"Bill Turner has turned his unique experience as litigator, teacher, and journalist into a masterful scholarly but eminently readable analysis of the Supreme Court's use of the First Amendment to advance a conservative political agenda. Rare is a book about law so jargon free."

—Michael Meltsner, Matthews University of Professor of Law at Northeastern School of Law and author of *The Making of a Civil Rights Lawyer*

"The First Amendment was intended to protect the dissident—the little guy—from the heavy hand of the government, but Turner shows how the recent Supreme Court has weaponized it on behalf of corporate interests. The court has equated corporations with "people," treated money like "speech," and forced ordinary Americans to fight an uphill battle. This is the kind of book that will make you angry and energized."

—Bill Petrocelli, author of *Through the Bookstore Window* and co-owner of Book Passage bookstore

WILLIAM BENNETT TURNER

FREE SPEECH
FOR SOME

How the Supreme Court Is Weaponizing
the First Amendment to Empower
Corporations and the Religious Right

ROARING FORTIES
PRESS

Berkeley, California

Roaring Forties Press
1053 Santa Fe Avenue
Berkeley, CA 94706
www.roaringfortiespress.com

Cover design by Nigel Quinney and Amy M. Inouye; interior design by Nigel Quinney.

Library of Congress Cataloging-in-Publication Data

Names: Turner, William Bennett, author.
Title: Free speech for some : how the Supreme Court is weaponizing the
  First amendment to empower corporations and the religious right /
  William Bennett Turner.
Description: Berkeley : Roaring Forties Press, 2019. | Includes
  bibliographical references and index. | Summary: "Has the First
  Amendment become a tool to promote the conservative agenda? On June 27,
  2018, Justice Elena Kagan, dissenting from the Supreme Court's decision
  in a free speech case, accused the Roberts Court majority of
  "weaponizing the First Amendment"—of "turning the First Amendment into
  a sword" and using it to serve a conservative political agenda. The U.S.
  Supreme Court under Chief Justice John G. Roberts, Jr., has decided more
  free speech cases than any previous court in history. The decisions have
  mostly favored free speech claims. But the court increasingly has found
  First Amendment protection not for dissidents and minorities but for
  businesses and conservative religious interests. The court has taken
  free speech principles developed decades ago to shield and empower
  oppressed minorities and applied them to shield and empower corporations
  and the religious right. The book critically examines how the Roberts
  Court has decided the key cases, changed the rules on free speech,
  engineered outcomes, and become the willing vehicle for advancing the
  conservative agenda. Justice Kagan was right"— Provided by publisher.
Identifiers: LCCN 2019025012 (print) | LCCN 2019025013 (ebook) | ISBN
  9781938901881 (paperback) | ISBN 9781938901898 (ebook)
Subjects: LCSH: Freedom of speech—United States. | Political questions and
  judicial power—United States.
Classification: LCC KF4772 .T866 2019 (print) | LCC KF4772 (ebook) | DDC
  342.7308/53—dc23
LC record available at https://lccn.loc.gov/2019025012
LC ebook record available at https://lccn.loc.gov/2019025013

To the memory of Anthony Lewis,
a great writer about the Supreme Court,
columnist, scholar, mentor, and inspiration

CONTENTS

A PERSONAL NOTE

We all say we believe in free speech, at least when it is our own or it expresses a point of view we agree with. When it is an idea that we loathe, our commitment may waver. My own commitment to the freedom of speech grew with my experience as a First Amendment lawyer, as a teacher, as a sometimes journalist, and, above all, as a citizen.

As a Lawyer

When I was a young civil rights lawyer working at the NAACP Legal Defense Fund in the late 1960s and early 1970s, besides school desegregation, employment discrimination, and fair housing cases, I happened into a newly developing area of the law: prisoners' rights. While this was before the mass incarceration era, prisons notoriously held a disproportionate number of African Americans, and the fund viewed establishing some minimal rights for prisoners as a logical extension of the civil rights movement. The problem was, at the time, most courts took a hands-off attitude toward prisoners' complaints, refusing to interfere with the discretion of prison officials. This most despised minority—prisoners—had virtually no rights a court would respect or enforce. But some of their claims could not be ignored. I handled the first prison-conditions case in the country to go to a full trial, and that earned me pen pals from lockups near and far. I ended up representing prison-

ers in several states in constitutional litigation against prison-
system conditions and rules.

The first case I argued in the US Supreme Court involved
California prison rules that prohibited prisoners, in their letters
to family and friends, from "unduly complaining," "magnify-
ing grievances," or saying anything "otherwise inappropriate."
A prisoner wrote to our office saying he had been disciplined
for violating these rules and asking if the rules were consistent
with the First Amendment. I hoped not, but this had never
been decided by a court. We sued. The court unanimously held
the rules unconstitutional.[1] My career as a free speech lawyer
was launched.

I argued two other cases in the court, wrote the briefs and
strategized on many more, and argued lots of cases in various
federal courts of appeals and state supreme courts. Over the
years, I was able to attract clients who were not incarcerated, a
few of whom could actually pay a fee. Most of the cases were
on behalf of nonprofit organizations and eccentrics whose
cases were of little interest to lawyers intent on making a lot
of money. But I believed the cases presented significant free
speech issues. For example, I represented a gay newspaper
whose news racks were raided and emptied by police on orders
of the chief of police who had been caricatured on the pa-
per's front page; a public television station seeking to televise
the first California execution in a generation; *Wired* magazine
when it was sued for libel by an abusive cult leader; a federal
convict punished for writing columns published by the *San
Francisco Chronicle*; local newspapers subjected to libel claims;
and an edgy political website challenging a federal law against
"indecent" online content.

Through this work I came to appreciate the judges who
were open minded and courageous enough to protect speech
that the majority of citizens found distasteful or despicable

and the judges who treated the freedom of speech as politically neutral, protective of Nazis, antiwar activists, religious fanatics, and civil rights demonstrators alike, allowing the powerless as well as the powerful to have their say—and to be heard. Not free speech for some, but for all.

As a Teacher

For thirty-three years, I have been teaching courses on freedom of speech and the press at the University of California, Berkeley, the cradle of the Free Speech Movement. I have now taught thousands of undergraduates and graduate journalism students what I know about the First Amendment. Every year I learn something new from my students and about free speech principles. Some students start the course with preconceived notions that the law is deadly dull, consisting of rules to memorize. A few believe free speech is an absolute. Or they believe the opposite: government should suppress unpatriotic speech, hate speech, deliberate lies, speech alleged to threaten national security, or speech that causes emotional distress. After reading some of the classic cases—for example, *New York Times v. Sullivan* and the "Pentagon Papers" case—lightbulbs go on. These cases are gifts that do not stop giving.[2] Some of the great Supreme Court opinions (of, e.g., Oliver Wendell Holmes and Louis Brandeis) stir feelings of patriotism.[3] Students begin to appreciate that we are one of the few countries in the world to enjoy these freedoms, which we owe to Supreme Court decisions.

As a Journalist

In the late 1970s and early 1980s, while still practicing law, I was the legal correspondent for KQED, the public broadcasting station in San Francisco. (I had also represented the station in a case in the Supreme Court.) When a Supreme Court decision came down, the station would send wire copy about the decision to my law office; I would try to make sense of it, write a script, and then hop on my bike to go to the studio to air my report on the news of the day. I also worked on investigative stories on legal controversies, as well as ten or so documentaries on the courts and a four-hour series on PBS on the bicentennial of the Constitution. Hanging around and working with journalists at the station, I learned how professionals care about finding the truth and telling it (no "fake news" here) and what freedom of "the press" means in practice.

I do not consider myself a journalist, but I have published two other books on the First Amendment and dozens of articles in magazines, newspapers, and online sites on subjects ranging from televising court proceedings to televising executions, from provocative free speech opinions to the Supreme Court's treatment of "indecent" speech on radio and television, from Internet issues to *Citizens United*, from the centennial of free speech decisions to the Roberts Court's most recent cases.[4] Trying to interpret the court and the legal system for the general public—in ways accessible to all—has been invaluable to me in understanding, and appreciating, the First Amendment and its values.

As a Citizen

We citizens ought to know our rights and where they come from, and we should never take them for granted. President Barack Obama said in his farewell address that "the most important office in a democracy" is "citizen."[5] Retired Supreme Court Justice Sandra Day O'Connor noted that most citizens know very little about their government and "knowledge about our government is not handed down through the gene pool. Every generation has to learn it, and we have some work to do."[6] She lamented that a strong majority of Americans knew at least one of the *American Idol* judges but hardly any could name the chief justice of the Supreme Court.

Paying attention to the decisions of the court is not a task to be handed off to lawyers. As this book will remind you, what the First Amendment means is what at least five current justices say it means. The only way we citizens can hold the unelected justices accountable is by knowing what they have decided and why. That is why I wrote this book.

The First Amendment, as it developed over the last century, served well to protect dissidents and to enrich our public discourse. We should be proud of our country's free speech tradition. But we should be concerned when courts convert revered free speech principles—traditionally used to protect the most vulnerable among us—into tools for achieving economic or religious goals. Nor should justices decide cases by applying their own partisan political, economic, or religious ideology.

I attempt in this book to report, accurately, the decisions that the justices on the Supreme Court under Chief Justice John G. Roberts, Jr. have rendered on what the First Amendment means and the impact these decisions have on us today and will have for many years to come.

A central goal of the First Amendment is to encourage the free exchange of ideas and criticisms of government and government officials, including judges. Mine are in the pages to follow. Feel free to disagree.

W. B. T.
Berkeley
August 2019

FREE SPEECH
FOR SOME

INTRODUCTION

On June 27, 2018, Justice Elena Kagan, dissenting from the Supreme Court's decision in a free speech case, accused the Roberts Court majority of "weaponizing the First Amendment," of "turning the First Amendment into a sword," and using it to serve a conservative political agenda.[1] The majority was deploying the amendment in a way that "unleashes judges, now and in the future, to intervene in economic and regulatory policy." Since "almost all economic and regulatory policy affects or touches speech," there would be "black-robed rulers overriding citizens' choices. The First Amendment was meant for better things." That's a serious accusation. Was she right?

The Roberts Court has decided more free speech cases than any court in history. The decisions have mostly favored free speech claims. But the court increasingly has found First Amendment protection not for the dissidents who historically needed the First Amendment to get their voices heard, but for corporations and conservative religious interests. The court has taken free speech principles developed decades ago to shield and empower oppressed citizens and applied them to shield and empower corporations and the Christian right.

The court's jurisdiction is discretionary.[2] It is not required to decide all of the cases presented to it. Each year the justices receive about eight thousand petitions imploring the court to review and decide cases. Each petition claims the case presents issues of national importance requiring resolution by the highest court in the land. It takes the vote of four justices to grant review (and, of course, a majority of five to decide a case). The justices pick and choose from the thousands of petitions and agree to hear only about seventy cases each year. (One's chances of "taking the case all the way to the Supreme Court" are less than 1 percent.) Without explaining why, the Roberts Court has elected to hear a disproportionate number of free speech cases. More and more of the cases accepted for decision involve claims by corporations, businesses, and the Christian right. And more and more of those claims succeed. As one empirical study concludes, "Corporations have increasingly displaced individuals as direct beneficiaries of First Amendment rights."[3]

*   *   *

The First Amendment means what at least five of the current justices say it means—no more and no less. Despite the absolute language of the First Amendment ("Congress shall make *no* law . . . abridging the freedom of speech"), it does not ensure the right to say whatever one wants, wherever and whenever one wants. The first Supreme Court case to say so—indeed, the court's first free speech decision, *Schenck v. United States*—came in 1919.[4] The court unanimously upheld the conviction of an antiwar pamphleteer who opposed the military draft and called for citizens to write their congressional representatives. The legendary justice Oliver Wendell Holmes, Jr. made the point that free speech is not an absolute with a vivid metaphor: "The most stringent protection of free speech would not protect a man in falsely shouting fire in a theatre and causing a panic." The "shouting fire" metaphor had no proper place in a case involving reasoned written criticism of government policies (rather than garden-variety disturbing the peace, a misdemeanor everywhere). But people continue to trot it out every time they confront speech they believe should be suppressed. Schenck, the hapless socialist pamphleteer, served six months in prison. Fortunately, Justice Holmes came to change his mind about free speech; his later opinions ultimately persuaded the court, and the American people, that subversive, unpatriotic, or offensive speech merited First Amendment protection. The *Schenk* outcome would be unthinkable today.

* * *

When Chief Justice John G. Roberts, Jr. was nominated in 2005 by President George W. Bush, he testified at his Senate confirmation hearing that judges should behave like "umpires," merely calling balls and strikes, with no agenda.[5] But as the decisions discussed in this book demonstrate, deciding First Amendment cases—presenting complex, value-laden issues with competing societal interests—is nothing like calling balls and strikes. When it comes to interpreting the Constitution in the twenty-first century, in a diverse society with amazing technologies, there is no strike zone. Deciding what is comprehended by "speech," what comes within "*the* freedom of speech,"[6] and whether it has been "abridged" is an exceedingly difficult job.

The Roberts Court is not a court composed of *judicial* conservatives. It is a court with a majority of five politically conservative men, all Republicans appointed by Republican presidents, who are judicial activists. Judicial conservatism traditionally has meant exercising restraint: being reluctant to overturn democratically enacted laws; deciding narrowly, not painting with too broad a brush; and respecting the precedents set in previously decided cases (the doctrine of stare decisis). But the Roberts Court has invalidated many federal, state, and even local laws and overruled decades-old precedents. A true judicial conservative, Justice Felix Frankfurter, complained in 1943 that the court had—for the first time ever—overruled a precedent in order to strike down a law passed by a democratically elected legislature.[7] Now, the Roberts Court does so regularly.

The Roberts Court, 2019. Front row (left to right): Justices Stephen Breyer, Clarence Thomas, John G. Roberts, Jr., Ruth Bader Ginsburg, and Samuel Alito. Back row: Justices Neil Gorsuch, Sonia Sotomayor, Elena Kagan, and Brett Kavanaugh.

* * *

Historically, the highest and best use of the First Amendment was to protect dissident political speech. Among the many "better things" the amendment was meant for, which Justice Kagan must have had in mind, were rulings that protected Jehovah's Witnesses schoolchildren who refused to recite the Pledge of Allegiance to the flag,[8] allowed a Communist camp counselor to lead a pledge of allegiance to a red hammer-and-sickle flag,[9] shielded anti–Vietnam War protesters and anti–

Reagan administration protesters from criminal prosecution,[10] protected a fascist whose incendiary speech aroused and angered his audience and protestors,[11] permitted Nazis to march in Skokie, Illinois,[12] allowed civil rights demonstrators to march to end racial segregation,[13] and said that the "central meaning" of the First Amendment is the right of the press and all citizens to criticize government and public officials.[14]

What was *not* meant as one of the "better things" is judicial intervention in economic and regulatory policy. That dubious distinction belonged to the Supreme Court in the "*Lochner* era," when the court routinely struck down social welfare legislation at the behest of big business. *Lochner v. New York*, decided in 1905,[15] invalidated a law capping the hours that could be worked by bakery employees (to ten hours a day and sixty a week). The court commandeered the Due Process Clause of the Fourteenth Amendment, which protected citizens against the deprivation of "liberty," and aggressively put it to use. The court said the state law unconstitutionally restricted the workers' "liberty of contract," their supposed right to contract with employers to work as long as they wished. The court, dominated by politically conservative justices, continued for decades to weaponize the Due Process Clause to strike down a wide variety of legislation protecting against big business excesses, including labor and minimum wage laws. After it ruled several of President Franklin D. Roosevelt's New Deal reforms unconstitutional, and Roosevelt's plan to "pack" the court with more reasonable justices failed, change in the composition of the court finally altered the court's direction.

The *Lochner* era is generally viewed as a disgraceful period in the court's history. None other than Chief Justice Roberts himself denounced the decision in his Senate confirmation hearing.[16] In his passionate dissent in the same-sex marriage case ten years later, Roberts accused the majority of reviving "the unprincipled tradition of judicial policymaking that characterized discredited decisions such as *Lochner*."[17] Roberts noted that in the *Lochner* era, the court "struck down nearly 200 laws as violations of individual liberty." He said *Lochner* was a "debacle" in which the justices were "converting their personal preferences into constitutional mandates" on social and economic issues. These were "naked policy preferences," and the court should never again revive "the grave errors of that period."

What Roberts was not willing to recognize was that his court is doing with the First Amendment the same thing the *Lochner* court did with the Due Process Clause. In the *Lochner* era, the court invoked an amendment intended to protect previously enslaved people—due process of law—to free business from unwelcome regulatory legislation. Now, the question is whether the court is weaponizing a different constitutional amendment, the First, to achieve the same antiregulatory goals—that is, whether a new *Lochner*-like effort is afoot.

* * *

Lochner's due process theory had been largely discredited by 1971. But that year the famous "Powell memo" inspired a new era of judicial activism on behalf of conservative interests.[18] On August 23, 1971, two months before he was nominated to the Supreme Court by President Richard Nixon, Lewis Powell wrote a memorandum to his friend Eugene Sydnor, an official at the US Chamber of Commerce. Powell was a prominent corporate lawyer in Richmond, Virginia. He served on several corporate boards, and among his clients were Philip Morris, Inc. and the Tobacco Institute.

Powell's memo lamented that "the American economic system is under broad attack." He said the "American business and enterprise system" was in grave jeopardy. "We are not dealing with sporadic or isolated attacks from a relatively few extremists or even from the minority socialist cadre. Rather, the assault on the enterprise system is broadly based and consistently pursued. It is gaining momentum and converts." Among the sources of the attacks were Ralph Nader, an assortment of "New Leftists," academics, the media, and politicians.

Powell urged the Chamber of Commerce to lead the battle to fight back. He said the chamber should enlist its corporate members to support a multifaceted campaign and to assume "a broader and more vigorous role in the political arena." The campaign would try to influence and control not just public perceptions of business but also antibusiness activity in government, academia, the media, and—importantly—the courts.

Powell said that "with an activist-minded Supreme Court, the judiciary may be the most important instrument for social, economic, and political change." He pointed to the success of "the most active exploiters of the judicial system," groups ranging in political orientation from "'liberal' to the far left." He cited the American Civil Liberties Union (ACLU) as an example of an organization that "initiates or intervenes in scores of cases each year." Labor unions, civil rights groups, and public interest law firms are "extremely active in the judicial arena," and "their success, often at business' expense, has not been inconsequential." Powell said the chamber should emulate these groups in using the courts to advance business interests.

The Powell memo spurred the chamber to action. It soon set up a National Chamber Litigation Center that began identifying cases that affect business interests, supporting them, and filing *amicus curiae* (friend of the court) briefs. It has been extraordinarily successful in the Roberts Court. In recent years, it has filed briefs in about a quarter of the cases on the court's docket, and it has prevailed in more than half of them.[19] It has also been adept in shaping the court's docket by identifying promising cases and flagging them for the court by filing *amicus* briefs urging the court to exercise its discretionary power to review them.

The Powell memo helped inspire the creation of other conservative advocacy organizations such as the Cato Institute (founded in 1974 by Charles Koch), the Pacific Legal Foundation (founded in 1973 by members of Ronald Reagan's staff), the Landmark Legal Foundation (1976), the Southeastern Legal Foundation (1976), and, more recently, Christian right organizations like Alliance Defending Freedom and First Liberty. All these organizations are committed to using the courts to serve their conservative political agendas. All have been aggressively developing cases seeking to move the law rightward. In the same ways the ACLU and the NAACP Legal Defense Fund worked to bring cases to change the law before the Powell memo, the conservative organizations are doing it today. The conservative litigators, however, are better funded and more disciplined ideologically than their liberal counterparts. They are getting a warm reception in the Roberts Court, while the liberal organizations are largely on the defensive.

*   *   *

So, who are the justices on the Roberts Court—the "black-robed rulers" (or "umpires") who decide what the First Amendment means? Justice Antonin Scalia, in his bitter dissent from the court's 2015 same-sex marriage decision,[20] described the justices on the Roberts Court, as "hardly a cross-section of America." He called them an elite, patrician "committee of nine unelected lawyers" who should not have been allowed, in the case he was complaining about, to exercise the power to declare longstanding marriage laws unconstitutional.

When Scalia wrote, the Roberts Court justices were even less representative of American demographics than he acknowledged. The court had six Catholics and three Jews. There was one African-American and one Latina; no Asian-American has ever served on the court. There were twice as many men as women. Every one of the justices went to Harvard Law School or Yale Law School. Almost all were well along in years. Four were natives of New York City. All but one had served on a federal court of appeals before being elevated to the court. None served on a state court or legislature, as a governor, or in Congress.

The recent addition of Neil Gorsuch and Brett Kavanaugh, two Catholic white men who went to Harvard and Yale, respectively, did not appreciably change those demographics.

Chief Justice John G. Roberts, Jr., and Justice Neil Gorsuch

All the court's conservative members (including the newest members, Gorsuch and Kavanaugh) were members of the Federalist Society,[21] an organization of "conservatives and libertarians" founded in 1982 to combat what they perceived as the liberal leanings of the nation's law schools and the courts.[22] The Federalist Society believes that "law schools and the legal profession are currently strongly dominated by a form of orthodox liberal ideology which advocates a centralized and uniform society." The Federalist Society attempts to identify, nurture, and mentor young conservatives and prepare them for judicial clerkships, careers combatting government overreaching, and, in many cases, becoming judges. During the Roberts Court years, the society has been phenomenally successful in influencing the selection of federal judges. Donald Trump used the society's list of twenty-one reliable conservatives as the sole source for his two appointments to the court.

Of the earlier Roberts Court members, Justices Scalia, Samuel Alito, Clarence Thomas, Anthony Kennedy, and Chief Justice Roberts all came to Washington to work in the administration of Ronald Reagan, whose credo was to "get government off the backs of business." In his inaugural address, Reagan famously said "Government is not the solution to our problem, government is the problem."[23] Largely fresh from law school, the young men who eventually became justices spent their formative years as lawyers in an environment committed to liberating American businesses from the burden of government regulation.[24]

Some conservative justices on the Roberts Court have espoused "originalist" theories for how they interpret the Constitution. The originalists, whose intellectual leader was Justice Scalia, say the Constitution should be interpreted as the framers would have understood it back in 1787. However, originalism does not show the way to First Amendment outcomes, because there is precious little information about what the framers actually meant to include within "the freedom of speech." Nor do the words of the First Amendment provide answers, or even clues, to resolving the precise free speech issues that come before the court. (The more liberal justices on the court say the Constitution is a living document, whose meaning evolves with changing times.)

* * *

Here's an introduction to the justices who serve or have served on the Roberts Court since its inception in 2005.[25]

Chief Justice John G. Roberts, Jr. was appointed by President George W. Bush in 2005; the court has been known as the "Roberts Court" since Roberts took his seat. He was fifty when appointed, the youngest chief justice since John Marshall in 1801. He replaced William Rehnquist, for whom he had clerked. After his clerkship, Roberts worked in the Reagan Administration. At his Senate confirmation hearing, besides saying judges should act like umpires, he said judges should exercise "judicial restraint," deciding cases as narrowly as possible. Not painting with too broad a brush would promote unanimity, so the court could speak with a more authoritative voice. And the court should maintain respect for precedent under the doctrine of stare decisis. (These judicial restraint principles were notoriously cast aside in the court's *Citizens United* and *Janus* decisions discussed in chapters 1 and 2.)

Roberts's voting record is politically quite conservative. He has voted with his fellow conservatives in almost every 5–4 case, including the Second Amendment guns case, *Citizens United*, and the Voting Rights Act case. He dissented in the court's gay marriage, abortion, and affirmative action cases. He did vote with the liberals to save Obamacare,[26] and in one campaign finance case, discussed in chapter 1.[27] In an interview after the retirement of Justice Anthony Kennedy, Roberts said "conservative" and "liberal" labels should not be applied to the justices. As an example, he said, "I'm probably the most aggressive defender of the First Amendment."[28]

Here are the court's conservatives, in order of their seniority on the court.

Clarence Thomas was appointed by President George H. W. Bush in 1991 to replace the great Thurgood Marshall, who had been the first African-American on the court.

Thomas has a compelling life story. He was born in poverty in Pin Point, Georgia. He studied for the priesthood and then miraculously made his way to Yale Law School. After graduation he worked in the pesticide division of Monsanto Corporation. He joined the Reagan Administration, where he served as head of the Equal Employment Opportunity Commission (EEOC; this is where he worked with Anita Hill, who testified at his confirmation hearing that Thomas sexually harassed her). Contrary to the EEOC's established positions, Thomas opposed affirmative action and the use of class actions in discrimination cases.

As a justice, Thomas has been the most politically conservative on the court. (His wife has been a Tea Party activist, causing some to complain that Thomas should recuse himself in cases involving contentious issues on which the Tea Party has staked a position.) Linda Greenhouse, former Supreme Court correspondent for the *New York Times* and a seasoned observer of the court, said Thomas "revels in his chosen role as the anti–Thurgood Marshall," viewing affirmative action as a "cruel farce," and the Voting Rights Act as insufficiently gutted by the court.[29]

Notoriously, Thomas almost never asks a question during oral arguments. But he writes more opinions than any other justice. Most are concurring and dissenting opinions giving voice to his idiosyncratic views. He rarely writes majority opinions in high-profile cases, possibly because his views are so extreme that he cannot convince a majority to sign on with him. He is an avowed originalist and never passes up the opportunity to reconstruct history in search of support for conservative outcomes. Linda Greenhouse again: Thomas is "a judge at war not only with modernity but with the entire project of constitutional law."[30]

On February 19, 2019, loner Thomas outdid himself. He seized on an opportunity to write an extended originalist opinion calling for the court to overrule *New York Times v. Sullivan,* probably the most important First Amendment decision in American history.[31] *Sullivan* was the case in which the court unanimously declared the "central meaning" of the First Amendment was the right we all have to criticize government and public officials without fear of being sued for libel. No party in the case in which Thomas elected to attack *Sullivan* had even mentioned *Sullivan.* Undeterred, Thomas gratuitously lambasted *Sullivan* and the many precedents applying it as "policy-driven decisions masquerading as constitutional law." His revisionist history and reasoning were not joined by any other justice.[32]

Samuel Alito was George W. Bush's second appointment, in 2006. He was Bush's second choice for the opening and was nominated when Harriet Miers withdrew. Alito had enthusiastically worked in the Reagan Justice Department as a young lawyer. In his job application he touted his conservative credentials and said, "the greatest influences on my views were the writings of William F. Buckley, Jr., the *National Review,* and

Barry Goldwater's 1964 campaign."[33] His appointment as a replacement for Sandra Day O'Connor, the first woman on the court, moved the political middle of the court significantly rightward, as Alito is a fairly rigid, doctrinaire political conservative. For example, he was the architect of the anti-union *Janus* decision discussed in chapter 2. He has consistently ruled in favor of business and religious right interests, including in First Amendment cases, and takes a very hard line on criminal cases, including the death penalty. In several of the court's more traditional free speech cases (chapter 6), Alito seemed to have found the speech morally offensive and dissented from First Amendment rulings.

Neil Gorsuch was Donald Trump's first appointment, nominated in 2017 to fill the opening left by Antonin Scalia's death. Gorsuch's name was drawn from the list of reliable conservative candidates supplied by the Federalist Society. He was confirmed by the Senate after the Republicans exercised the "nuclear option" to allow confirmation by a simple majority rather than sixty votes. Before clerking for Justice Anthony Kennedy, Gorsuch earned an Oxford degree in philosophy, wrote his thesis on assisted suicide, and met and married his English wife.

Gorsuch was a great admirer of Justice Scalia and his approach to judging. Unlike the older conservative justices, he did not serve in the Reagan administration (he was in high school then), but his mother did, as administrator of the Environmental Protection Agency.[34]

Shortly after his confirmation, Gorsuch gave a speech at a Federalist Society dinner—in the new Trump Hotel in Washington—in which he proclaimed, "Tonight I can report, a person can be both a committed originalist and textualist and be confirmed to the Supreme Court of the United States.

Thank you from the bottom of my heart for your support and prayers through that process." He added that "Originalism has regained its place and textualism has triumphed and neither is going anywhere on my watch. . . . In our legal system, judges wear robes, not capes."

Brett Kavanaugh was Trump's second nominee. He had a contentious confirmation hearing when allegations of sexual abuse and drinking surfaced. He was narrowly confirmed on July 9, 2018. He went to the same Catholic high school as Neil Gorsuch, but then to Yale Law School rather than Harvard. After clerking for Justice Kennedy, Kavanaugh worked for independent counsel Kenneth Starr on the Bill Clinton–Monica Lewinsky report. He also worked for the George W. Bush administration, first on *Bush v. Gore,* the case in which the court gave the 2000 election to Bush.[35] He then served as White House counsel and then staff secretary.

Justice Brett Kavanaugh and Donald Trump at Kavanaugh's swearing-in.

Kavanaugh was appointed by Bush to the District of Columbia Circuit Court of Appeals. His many opinions in the appellate court showed fairly consistent political conservatism. His replacement of Kennedy probably moved the court in a more conservative direction on issues like abortion, affirmative action, same-sex marriage, and the death penalty. It is unclear whether Kavanaugh will be as strong on the First Amendment as Kennedy was. The Kennedy-Kavanaugh swap left Chief Justice Roberts as the man in the middle with the swing vote, an indication of how conservative the court has become.

Here are the current court's liberal justices, in order of their seniority on the court.

Ruth Bader Ginsburg was named to the court by President Bill Clinton in 1993. She grew up in a working-class Jewish neighborhood in Brooklyn. After law school she taught at Rutgers and then worked for the ACLU Women's Rights Project, where she argued several key employment and women's rights cases before the court.

"The Notorious RBG" has become something of a folk hero, the subject of both a documentary film and a feature movie in 2018. Despite her age (eighty-six in 2019) and her bouts with cancer, she speaks widely and candidly about her work on the court (and her fitness workouts). During the late Obama years, when she was asked if she would retire and give Obama the appointment, she said no one as liberal as she could be confirmed by a Republican Senate, and so she would hang on. Indeed, her voting record on the court is consistently liberal and, as of this writing, she's still hanging on.

Stephen Breyer, a native San Franciscan, was also appointed by Bill Clinton. He worked for the Antitrust Division of the

Justice Department and for Senator Ted Kennedy on the Senate Judiciary Committee. Airline deregulation was one of his efforts. He taught at Harvard Law School for many years before being appointed by President Jimmy Carter to the First Circuit Court of Appeals.

Breyer's wife is British, and he is a bit of an Anglophile and internationalist. He, more than other justices, looks at how other countries handle controversial issues. (This infuriated Justice Antonin Scalia, who thought the American Constitution and laws should be the sole source for all the answers.) Breyer is also a compromiser, always searching for a reasonable, pragmatic way to accommodate the competing interests in a case. He has developed views about First Amendment adjudication that are much more flexible than the Roberts Court's doctrinaire approach, and he has strenuously objected to the court's using the amendment to upset routine business regulation.

Sonia Sotomayor was President Barack Obama's first appointee and the first Latina to join the court. Sotomayor, like Clarence Thomas, has a compelling life story, very different from the more privileged justices on the court. Puerto Rican, she grew up in a housing project in the Bronx and made her way to Yale Law School. A lifelong Democrat, she was—back when bipartisanship was possible—named to the federal trial bench by the first President Bush. Then she was elevated to the Second Circuit Court of Appeals by Bill Clinton. While there, she gave a talk at the University of California, Berkeley, in which she said, "I would hope that a wise Latina woman in the richness of her experience would more often" reach a better decision "than a white man who hasn't lived that life." She of course had to dial that back in her confirmation hearing when Obama appointed her to the court in 2009.[36]

Sotomayor is a genuine liberal. She brings her lived experience to the court's deliberations. She is strong on the libertarian aspects of the First Amendment but opposed to its use to serve the interests of businesses, conservatives, and the religious right.

Justice Sonia Sotomayor and President Barack Obama.

Elena Kagan became President Obama's second appointment. After law school at Harvard, she clerked for Thurgood Marshall. She worked for a Washington law firm, and then taught at the University of Chicago, where she was a colleague of Barack Obama. While there, she wrote a scholarly law review article trying to make sense of the court's First Amendment jurisprudence, and she still tries to get the majority justices to invoke the amendment only when necessary to serve the need to protect core political and dissident speech.

Kagan served in the Clinton Administration and then was nominated to the DC Court of Appeals, but Republicans stalled the nomination until the 2000 election and it lapsed. Instead, she became the first woman dean of Harvard Law School. While dean, she hired then-judge Brett Kavanaugh to teach courses. In 2009, Obama tapped her to serve as solicitor general of the United States, the government's lawyer in the Supreme Court. She had never argued a case there. Her first argument was the *Citizens United* case. Obama appointed her to the Supreme Court shortly thereafter. At her confirmation hearing, Senator Lindsey Graham asked her where she had been on a certain Christmas Day. She responded, to laughter, "Like all Jews I was probably at a Chinese restaurant."

Kagan is the only current justice not to have served on a federal court of appeals. Her approach to judging—both asking probing questions at argument and crafting readable, plain-spoken opinions—is consistently practical and down to earth. She, like Justice Breyer, opposes the Roberts Court's use of the First Amendment to relieve businesses from economic regulation.

Here are the justices who formerly served on the Roberts Court.

Justice Antonin Scalia was the most colorful character on the court. He was a brilliant man, garrulous, engaging. He was the most prolific questioner during oral arguments, often dominating the proceedings and intimidating lawyers whose positions he disagreed with. He did not hide his feelings. He was a great writer, though caustic and confrontational in his dissents. One liberal First Amendment scholar said upon Scalia's death that "he was influential, not because he was right, but because he could write."[37]

Scalia was appointed in 1986 by President Ronald Reagan and served thirty years on the court. At his Senate confirmation hearing, to avoid creating controversy about his constitutional views, he refused to answer questions about any cases, saying "I do not think I should answer any questions regarding any specific Supreme Court opinion, even one as fundamental as *Marbury v. Madison.*" (*Marbury* was the seminal 1801 decision in which the court held it had the power of "judicial review," authorizing it to declare laws passed by Congress unconstitutional.) Scalia was the first Italian-American justice on the court. He was a devout Catholic and the father of nine children.

Scalia was very conservative politically, adamantly opposed to abortion, same-sex marriage, and the rights of gay people generally. He opposed affirmative action in education and any form of campaign finance reform. He was a strong proponent of the death penalty. He wrote the court's opinion declaring that the Second Amendment provided an individual right to own guns. He opposed many attempts by government to impose environmental and consumer regulations on business. He was antiunion. He was viewed by candidate Donald Trump as the "model" for how Supreme Court justices should rule.

When Scalia died unexpectedly in February 2016, President Obama nominated Court of Appeals Judge Merrick Garland to replace him. Garland was a highly qualified moderate whose credentials and experience were impeccable. But Senate Republicans under the leadership of Mitch McConnell refused even to give Garland a hearing.[38] After the election of 2016, the Garland nomination died. President Trump then appointed Neil Gorsuch to replace Scalia.

Anthony Kennedy was appointed by President Reagan in 1988. A Catholic from Sacramento, he had worked for Reagan when he was governor.

For much of his thirty-year tenure on the court, and all of his time on the Roberts Court, Kennedy was a key swing vote. He mostly sided with the conservative justices but occasionally, and unpredictably, voted with the more liberal justices in 5–4 decisions. On the Roberts Court, he voted with the liberals in 5–4 decisions about a quarter of the time, including in gay marriage, abortion, and affirmative action cases. Kennedy was essentially the decider in most high-profile cases: as Kennedy went, so went the court.

Kennedy was the Roberts Court's most enthusiastic supporter—and expander—of First Amendment freedoms. His opinions were characterized by over-the-top flowery rhetoric about free speech values. This includes his opinions in *Citizens United* and other cases in which he invoked the First Amendment as the basis for advancing conservative interests. One critic said upon Kennedy's retirement in June 2018 that Kennedy showed "neither humility nor rigor in his ultimate decisions —overruling state and federal law more frequently than any justice to his right or left, pontificating in sweeping and self-righteous and faux-poetic prose."[39] President Trump nominated Brett Kavanaugh, who had clerked for Kennedy out of law school, to replace him.

John Paul Stevens was President Gerald Ford's only appointment, in 1975. A moderate Republican, Stevens took some years to find his First Amendment sensibilities. He wrote an unfortunate opinion in a case establishing the Federal Communications Commission's power to censor and punish broadcasters who aired "indecent" material (e.g., comedian George Carlin's famous Seven Dirty Words monologue).[40] But he moved steadily leftward during his thirty-five-year tenure on the court and qualified as a bona fide, principled, consistent liberal by the time he retired in 2010. As his parting shot, he wrote the ninety-page magisterial dissent in *Citizens United*. After his retirement, he candidly criticized decisions he strongly disagreed with, singling out *Bush v. Gore*, the Second Amendment gun decision, and *Citizens United*. He had dissented in all three.

David Souter, like Stevens, was a moderate Republican. Appointed by President George H. W. Bush in 1990, Souter became more liberal during his tenure, to the chagrin of conservatives who had been assured of his conservative reliability. A lifelong bachelor and something of a recluse, he disliked being in Washington. Once asked when the court would permit televised arguments, he said, "the day you see a camera come into our courtroom, it is going to roll over my dead body."[41] He opposed invoking the First Amendment to invalidate campaign finance regulations, dissenting in several cases and writing a draft dissent in *Citizens United* that caused the majority to defer deciding the case until after Souter's retirement. He was a strong believer in First Amendment protection for dissident speech. He retired at the end of the term in 2009 and retreated to rural New Hampshire. Conservatives vowed never to nominate "another Souter." Indeed, the Republican appointees since Souter's retirement, Gorsuch and Kavanaugh, have been Federalist Society–vetted ideological conservatives, not moderates.

Sandra Day O'Connor, appointed by Ronald Reagan and the first woman on the court, was ever-so-briefly a member of the Roberts Court. She announced her retirement on July 1, 2005. George W. Bush nominated John Roberts to succeed her. But then Chief Justice William Rehnquist died, and Bush decided to appoint Roberts as chief. O'Connor stayed on the court until January 31, 2006, when she was replaced by Samuel Alito. That swap, Alito for O'Connor, moved the court sharply in a more conservative direction, as O'Connor was a moderate on many issues, and Alito is not. O'Connor did not participate in

President Ronald Reagan and Justice Sandra Day O'Connor.

any significant First Amendment cases in the few months she served on the Roberts Court.

*   *   *

This book reveals, in case after case, how the politically conservative Roberts Court justices have fashioned or extended First Amendment rules, engineered outcomes, and converted the amendment into an important weapon in the conservative political arsenal. The starting point is *Citizens United*, the Roberts Court's signature decision, granting corporations a First Amendment right to spend without limit on elections. Then comes *Janus*, capping the conservatives' concerted campaign to disable and take political power away from public employee unions. Following is an examination of the court's other business-friendly decisions. The Roberts Court has consistently favored American businesses, often shielding them from consumer, financial, and environmental regulations. This has now carried over into the First Amendment arena, with the court using free speech principles as antiregulatory tools.

Next are cases brought by religious fundamentalists who oppose same-sex marriage and abortion and who invoke free speech principles to achieve their ends.

While they have enthusiastically used the First Amendment to favor corporate and Christian right interests, the Roberts Court justices have ruled against free speech claims made by school students, military personnel, government employees, and prisoners. The court has not satisfactorily explained why these groups of human beings do not have full First Amendment protection, while corporations do.

Finally, the book looks at the court's more traditional free speech rulings, cases in which the court has found First Amendment protection for hateful or obnoxious speech that most Americans find repugnant. These decisions do not single out corporations or the religious right for favored treatment, though the beneficiaries of the rulings include religious fundamentalists, businesses selling violent materials, and the Tea Party. In these and other cases, the court has muddied First Amendment analysis—the principles used to determine in which cases speech is either protected or can be suppressed.

The Roberts Court's free speech jurisprudence is confused and inconsistent. One of the few predictable themes is the court's willingness to use the First Amendment as the vehicle for expanding the rights of American business and the Christian right. The court's discovery of these new uses for the First Amendment is disillusioning for traditional free speech advocates, and it raises the question of whether it is time to reexamine what should be included in "the freedom of speech."

1

CITIZENS UNITED

Corporate Money Talks

Citizens United v. Federal Election Commission[1] is the Roberts Court's most important First Amendment decision. It is also the most misunderstood (partly because the opinions in the case run to 176 pages, and few people have read them). It freed corporations to spend without limit to support or oppose candidates for political office.

The *Citizens United* decision is in many ways the best example of what the Roberts Court has been doing with the First Amendment:

- It was a 5–4 decision, with the justices divided along familiar conservative-liberal lines according to the party of the president who appointed them.

- The majority opinion was written by Justice Anthony Kennedy, the court's most enthusiastic First Amendment supporter and the author of several of its most important free speech decisions.

- The result strongly advanced corporate and conservative political interests.

- Abandoning any commitment to judicial restraint, the court converted a narrow dispute into a major change in American law, overruled a long-standing precedent to arrive at the desired result, and delivered the broadest ruling imaginable.

• The court aggressively employed merciless, unforgiving scrutiny to the justifications offered by the government for restricting corporate spending.

• The decision had significant real-world consequences, greatly increasing the amount of money spent on political campaigns and creating new sources for campaign funding. Its reasoning led almost immediately to the creation of super PACs (political action committees). Although the court did not actually say, "money is speech," it held that "independent expenditures"—spending on elections not coordinated with a candidate—are incapable of causing corruption, are treated as "speech," and are therefore protected by the First Amendment. Today, more money goes into elections from independent expenditures than from contributions to candidates.

The decision was not a surprise.

*   *   *

The foundation for the decision was laid by the 1971 Powell memo; the result was engineered forty years later by the Roberts Court.

Beyond the memo's call for conservative activism, Lewis Powell contributed more directly to the ultimate *Citizens United* ruling when he became a justice of the Supreme Court. He authored the majority opinion in a 1978 case called *First National Bank of Boston v. Bellotti*.[2] A Massachusetts law prohibited corporations from spending to oppose a ballot proposition that would establish a state income tax. A group of corporations challenged the law as a violation of their First Amendment right of free speech. This presented a major undecided issue: Do corporations have First Amendment rights? Justice Powell artfully dodged it, saying the question was not whether corporations "have" First Amendment rights, but whether the law

Justice Lewis Powell, 1976.

"abridges expression that the First Amendment was meant to protect." The corporations proposed to engage in core political speech about an election, and this was speech "at the heart of the First Amendment protection." The question, therefore, was "whether the corporate identity of the speaker deprives this proposed speech of what would otherwise be its clear entitlement to protection." Powell's answer was no. In other words, the First Amendment protects the speech regardless of the corporate identity of the speaker. This became one of the major themes of the *Citizens United* decision.

So, What Was the Citizens United Case About?

Back when bipartisan congressional action was possible, Republican John McCain and Democrat Russ Feingold collaborated on a bill called the Bipartisan Campaign Reform Act of 2002. Known as the McCain-Feingold law, it contained a provision that prohibited both corporations and unions from using their funds on communications—mainly television advertising—that support or oppose a candidate for federal office. The law covered all corporations, small and large, nonprofit as well as for profit; it did exempt media corporations.

In 1990, in *Austin v. Michigan Chamber of Commerce*,[3] the court had upheld a very similar provision against constitutional attack. Michigan law barred corporations from making independent expenditures supporting or opposing candidates for state office. The Michigan Chamber of Commerce, itself a nonprofit corporation, challenged the law as a violation of its First Amendment rights. Justice Thurgood Marshall wrote the opinion for the 6–3 majority, upholding the law as serving the state's interest in preventing corruption or the appearance of corruption. Justices Antonin Scalia and Anthony Kennedy filed spirited dissents.

Austin was the law when McCain-Feingold passed and until the court handed down *Citizens United*.

* * *

Citizens United is a nonprofit corporation that engages in conservative advocacy. During the 2008 presidential primary campaign, it produced a ninety-minute documentary film called *Hillary: The Movie*. It was an attack on Hillary Clinton. As characterized by the court, the film was "a feature-length negative advertisement that urges viewers to vote against Senator Clinton for President." (Citizens United's president and producer of the film, David Bossie, later earned a position as Donald Trump's deputy campaign manager.) Citizens United released the film in some theaters and on DVD but wanted to increase distribution by putting it on cable television using video on demand (VOD). Fearing that doing so might violate the McCain-Feingold law, Citizens United sued the Federal Election Commission (FEC), seeking a determination that showing its film was not illegal.

Citizens United argued that the McCain-Feingold provision on electioneering by corporations did not apply to its movie. The provision was targeted at television political ads, not feature length films or VOD. And Citizens United contended the law did not apply to *it*, a nonprofit whose donors were mostly individuals. In the trial court, Citizens United formally stipulated that it was challenging the law only as applied to it and its film; it was not challenging the constitutionality of the law "on its face"—that is, as it might restrict any corporation and any ad. The trial court ruled against Citizens United, finding that the law applied and did not violate the First Amendment. Citizens United appealed.

The Supreme Court heard arguments twice, first on March 24, 2009. The experienced practitioner representing Citizens United, Theodore Olson, tried to win by persuading the justices to decide the case narrowly. His position stuck to the modest contentions made by Citizens United in the trial court: the provision of the McCain-Feinberg law did not apply to a full-length feature or VOD, as opposed to television commercials, and it did not apply to a nonprofit advocacy group like Citizens United. He did not suggest overruling the *Austin* decision or any other precedent.

When the justices met to deliberate after the argument, they voted 5–4 in the corporation's favor, and Chief Justice John Roberts assigned the writing of the majority opinion to himself. (The court's practice is that, when the chief justice is in the majority, he designates who will write the majority opinion. This is a significant power of the chief justice, as he or she may be able to influence how the case will be decided, and what kind of precedent it will set, by choosing one or another justice as the author.)

Roberts circulated to the justices a draft that decided the case on narrow grounds. But Justice Kennedy, supported by the other conservatives, then circulated a concurring opinion that broadly condemned the law on its face (in all its possible applications), rejected any narrow approach to deciding the case, and called for overruling *Austin* and any other precedents in the way. Apparently persuaded, Roberts then agreed to sign on and make the Kennedy version the majority opinion. That caused Justice David Souter, in his last term on the court before his retirement, to draft an uncharacteristically scathing dissent claiming the court was violating its own rules by deciding the case on grounds not raised by any party. In response, the majority justices decided to withhold any decision and set the case for reargument at a special session on September 9, 2009, after Souter's departure. The court ordered the parties to submit briefs on whether the court should overrule the 1990 *Austin* case. The writing was on the wall.[4]

As President Obama's solicitor general, Elena Kagan presented the second argument for the government. It was her first appellate argument in any court. She performed valiantly, in damage-control mode, but how the justices would rule was a foregone conclusion. On January 21, 2010, the court handed down its decision, holding that the McCain-Feingold law violated the First Amendment.

The Majority Decision

In order to find the McCain-Feingold law unconstitutional, Justice Kennedy's majority opinion had to jump over several analytical hurdles. Here are the steps in the court's logic.

The Case Should Not Be Decided Narrowly

First, the Kennedy opinion disposed of the contentions that would have allowed the court to decide the case narrowly and without invalidating the law on its face. The majority refused to read the law as not applying to the *Hillary* film, or to VOD, or to a nonprofit's political speech funded mostly by individuals. Any of these contentions would have allowed Citizens United to win without having the law held unconstitutional across the board. Justice Kennedy also brushed off the fact that Citizens United had stipulated in the trial court to forego its challenge to the law on its face and rely only on its arguments about how the law applied to it. Kennedy asserted, without acknowledging the irony, that the court must, "in an exercise of its judicial responsibility," determine whether the law was unconstitutional on its face. Otherwise, Kennedy said, "the substantial, nation-wide chilling effect" of the prohibition would be prolonged.[5]

The court has often struck down laws that it says create a "chilling effect" on speech, causing people to self-censor and refrain from saying what they want to say. The laws are usually broad and uncertain and often treat the forbidden speech as a criminal offense, deterring would-be speakers from taking the risk of saying what they want to say. The majority in *Citizens United* found a chilling effect in the uncertainty about exactly what communications the government would say were prohibited. The campaign finance regulations were exceedingly complex, and the FEC had adopted 568 pages of regulations, 1,278 pages of explanations and 1,771 advisory opinions. Kennedy said, "If parties want to avoid litigation and the possibility of civil and criminal penalties, they must either refrain from speaking or ask the FEC to issue an advisory opinion approving of the speech in question. . . . This is an unprecedented governmental intervention into the realm of speech."

The Law's Criminal Penalties Are Serious

The law covered all the millions of American corporations, including mom-and-pop operations, small single-shareholder companies, and nonprofits. Spending to support or oppose a candidate would subject all these kinds of corporations to criminal liability, accentuating the law's chilling effect. Kennedy observed that the law "makes it a felony for all corporations—including nonprofit advocacy corporations—either to expressly advocate the election or defeat of candidates or to broadcast electioneering communications within 30 days of a primary election and 60 days of a general election." Thus, organizations like the Sierra Club, the National Rifle Association, and the American Civil Liberties Union—all corporations—would commit felonies if they supported or opposed candidates whose positions they favored or abhorred.

(Raising troubling but hypothetical applications is apt only if the court is considering a challenge to the law on its face, as enforceable against anyone and any speech, rather than just as applied to Citizens United and its film.)

Spending Is "Speech"

The court had to treat spending on elections as "speech," or else the First Amendment would not apply. Contrary to popular understanding of the *Citizens United* decision, the court did not actually say "Money is speech." Instead, the court simply quoted from its seminal 1976 decision in *Buckley v. Valeo*[6] to the effect that any restriction on the amount of money spent on a political campaign "necessarily reduces the quantity of expression, . . . the number of issues discussed, the depth of their exploration and the size of the audience reached." (*Buckley* came in the post-Watergate attempt to reform campaign finance. It held that government could limit direct *contributions* to candidates, as this might lead to corruption or the appearance of corruption, but it did not apply this reasoning to "independent expenditures"—spending not coordinated with a campaign. It also recognized that rich politicians could spend as much as they wished on their own campaigns and people generally could independently spend without limit. The case did not involve corporate campaign spending.) The court in *Citizens United* did not view it as controversial that limiting spending restricted "speech" and therefore implicated the First Amendment. Accordingly, Justice Kennedy devoted no attention or analysis to whether expenditures *should* be considered speech.

Kennedy noted that the First Amendment "has its fullest and most urgent application to speech uttered during a campaign for public office." As Justice Powell had said in *Bellotti*, core political speech is the First Amendment's first concern. McCain-Feingold limited spending, and therefore speech, about candidates and issues.

"Strict Scrutiny" Should Be Applied

Under recognized First Amendment principles, laws restricting political speech based on its content are subject to "strict scrutiny" by the court. This requires the government to prove to the court's satisfaction that any restriction "furthers a compelling interest and is narrowly tailored to achieve that interest." The court exercises strict scrutiny when a law restricts speech on the basis of its content or message (as opposed to its time, place, or manner). The McCain-Feingold law indisputably restricted supporting or opposing candidates—the content of the speech, not where or how it was delivered. When the court applies strict scrutiny, it almost always throws out the restriction. It demands proof that the government's interests are not just important, or reasonable, but "compelling." And it demands evidence that the restriction is "narrowly tailored" in the sense that, for example, it does not restrict more speech than necessary to serve the government interests. Justice Kennedy aggressively employed the most rigorous scrutiny to the government's justifications for limiting corporate electioneering.

It Is the Speech, Not the Speaker, That Counts

Justice Kennedy's emphasis throughout his opinion was on the importance of protecting political *speech* regardless of who may be the *speaker*. He relied heavily on Lewis Powell's decision in *Bellotti*, emphasizing "*Bellotti*'s central principle: that the First Amendment does not allow political speech restrictions based on a speaker's corporate identity." Stating that "the Court has recognized that First Amendment protection extends to corporations," Justice Kennedy cited twenty-four historic First Amendment decisions, including landmarks like *New York Times v. Sullivan*[7] and the "Pentagon Papers" case,[8] all of which involved speech by corporations. (Almost all except *Bellotti* involved media corporations.) Under the cases, Kennedy said, "political speech does not lose First Amendment protection simply because its source is a corporation."

Kennedy had to acknowledge that the court had previously decided that certain categories of speakers—school students, government employees, military personnel, and prisoners—did not have full First Amendment rights, even for political speech. He summarily dismissed those limitations by saying they "were based on an interest in allowing governmental entities to perform their functions." He made no attempt to distinguish those cases or explain why the "government entities" involved could not function if the individuals had full free speech rights. It remains a mystery why corporations should have greater free speech rights than the individual human beings in these categories. If it is the speech that is protected regardless of the identity of the speaker, then there is no basis for favoring corporations over natural-person speakers. (See the discussion of disfavored speakers in chapter 5.)

Revealing his probusiness bent, Justice Kennedy remarked that the McCain-Feingold law "muzzled the voices that best represent the most significant segments of the economy," and "on certain topics corporations may possess valuable expertise, leaving them the best equipped to point out errors."

Citizens United protesters, Knoxville.

The Government's Interests Do Not Justify the Restrictions

Justice Kennedy rejected the government's justifications for the McCain-Feingold restrictions. The government contended that three different rationales supported restrictions on corporate speech in political campaigns: the "antidistortion" rationale, the "corruption or appearance of corruption" rationale, and the "protection of dissenting shareholders" rationale. Kennedy said two of the rationales were simply illegitimate and none justified the ban on corporate spending in elections.

The "Antidistortion" Rationale. What the court called the "antidistortion" rationale was used by the court in the 1990 *Austin* case as the basis for upholding the Michigan law. The idea was to "level the playing field" to prevent "the corrosive and distorting effects" on the political process of "immense aggregations of wealth that are accumulated with the help of the corporate form." Kennedy found this rationale was illegitimate. The McCain-Feingold law applied to nonprofit corporations and small (even single-shareholder) corporations that have not amassed any wealth and could not possibly tilt an election outcome. Justice Kennedy noted that there are 5.8 million for-profit corporations, most of which are relatively small businesses that do not have vast resources to spend on elections. Moreover, the antidistortion rationale would allow the government to ban all corporate political speech, even books. It would allow government to ban political speech of media corporations.

The main point, however, was that under *Buckley v. Valeo,* the 1976 campaign finance case, government had no legitimate business trying to "level the playing field." Justice Kennedy quoted from *Buckley:* "The concept that government may restrict the speech of some elements of our society in order to enhance the relative voice of others is wholly foreign to the First Amendment." In other words, government cannot ban the speech of rich and powerful entities or persons to keep them from drowning out those without comparable resources.

(In a speech,[9] the newest member of the Roberts Court, Brett Kavanaugh, called this quote from *Buckley* "one of the most important sentences in First Amendment history," perhaps telegraphing his view on the issues involved in *Citizens United* and future campaign finance cases.)

The "Corruption or Appearance of Corruption" Rationale. The *Buckley* decision used the "corruption" rationale to uphold restrictions on direct contributions to candidates for office. The reasoning was that large contributions could be given in anticipation of a political quid pro quo that would probably escape detection, so the restrictions ensured against the reality or appearance of corruption. The *Buckley* court, however, did not extend this rationale to independent political expenditures, and Justice Kennedy refused to do so. He acknowledged that preventing corruption is a legitimate government interest. But he noted that twenty-six states did not restrict independent expenditures and the government did not claim that this had corrupted the political process in those states. While there may be an "appearance of influence or access" stemming from independent spending on behalf of candidates, this "will not cause the electorate to lose faith in our democracy." Moreover, "ingratiation and access . . . are not corruption."

The court's concept of corruption is exceedingly narrow. It is limited to quid pro quo exchanges—essentially bribery. Moreover, the court said "independent expenditures" are incapable of corrupting. Spending not actually coordinated with a candidate's campaign—no matter how much influence, access, and

Justice Anthony Kennedy.

gratitude it buys—is speech protected by the First Amendment and beyond the legitimate reach of government regulation.

These willfully naïve pronouncements—no corruption without a quid pro quo, and independent expenditures cannot corrupt—are the linchpin of the court's reasoning. They are also the death knell for campaign finance reform. They betray not only ignorance of political realities but also the kind of judicial arrogance that led the court in the *Lochner* era to exalt a supposed "liberty of contract" over the reality of working conditions and invalidate dozens of laws opposed by business.

Justice Kennedy did not satisfactorily explain why the government's only valid interest is limited to blatant corruption, nor why independent expenditures are sacrosanct. Buying a legislator's gratitude and ear may not qualify as outright corruption, but there is no good reason why purchasing undue influence should be immune from reasonable congressional and state regulation. Nor is there reason to think that allowing corporations to buy "ingratiation and access" is good for democracy.

The "Protection of Minority Shareholders" Rationale. Justice Kennedy found the "shareholder protection" rationale even weaker than the government's other contentions. The idea here was to shield dissenting shareholders from, in effect, being compelled to fund corporate political speech with which they disagree. But Justice Kennedy pointed out that this rationale would allow government to ban the political speech of even media corporations. Moreover, there is little evidence of abuse that cannot be corrected, he said, through "corporate democracy" (another naïve notion of how the world works). And Kennedy pointed out that the law covers *all* corporations, including nonprofits and sole-shareholder companies with no minority shareholders to protect.

Austin Must Be Overruled

A centuries-old fundamental principle of Anglo-American law requires courts to follow the holdings of previously decided cases. This is known as the doctrine of stare decisis. This respect for precedent has always been acknowledged by the Supreme Court, and the court abides by it unless there are exceptional circumstances that justify overruling a previously decided case on point (i.e., a decision ruling on undistinguishable facts and the same legal issue).

Having found that *Austin* had relied on the illegitimate government "antidistortion" interest and defined corruption too loosely, the majority concluded *Austin* was simply wrong and must be overruled. The majority concluded: "We return to the principle" of previous decisions like *Bellotti* "that the government may not suppress political speech on the basis of the speaker's corporate identity." *Austin* was overruled and McCain-Feingold was unconstitutional on its face.

Roberts's Concurring Opinion

Chief Justice Roberts, apparently concerned about the seeming inconsistency between the majority's decision and his testimony at his 2005 confirmation hearing about respect for stare decisis and the need for judicial restraint (deciding cases on the narrowest grounds, not reaching out to decide broad issues that need not be resolved on the facts of the case, promoting unanimity among the justices, etc.), filed a concurring opinion to "address the important principles of judicial restraint and *stare decisis* implicated in this case."

Roberts agreed with the majority that there was no valid basis for deciding in Citizens United's favor without reaching the broad constitutional issue, and he said, "we cannot embrace a narrow ground of decision simply because it is narrow; it must also be right."

As for stare decisis, Roberts continued, it is not an "inexorable command . . . especially in constitutional cases." If it were, "segregation would be legal, minimum wage laws would be unconstitutional, and the government could wiretap ordinary criminal suspects without first obtaining warrants." (The court's precedents on those points had been overruled, as in, for example, *Brown v. Board of Education*.)[10] *Austin* was wrong and should be overruled. "When considering whether to reexamine a prior erroneous holding, we must balance the importance of having constitutional questions *decided* against the importance of having them *decided right*."[11]

The Stevens-Scalia Duel

Justice John Paul Stevens, who was then almost ninety years old, filed an extraordinary ninety-page dissent, joined by Justices Ruth Bader Ginsburg, Stephen Breyer, and Sonia Sotomayor. It characterized the majority opinion as simplistic, result oriented, and doctrinaire. The Stevens dissent was a painstaking, close reading of all the court's precedents and an intellectually rigorous, nuanced examination of campaign finance history, political realities, and the relevant interests.

Stevens began by emphasizing how little was really at stake for Citizens United. "The real issue in this case concerns how, not if," Citizens United "may finance its electioneering." It could televise the *Hillary* movie wherever and whenever it wanted except in the thirty days before the primary election. "All the parties dispute is whether Citizens United had a right to use the funds in its general treasury to pay for broadcasts during the 30-day period." In Stevens's view, the court improperly converted this narrow dispute into a "manufactured" facial attack on campaign finance laws that will "undermine the integrity of elected institutions across the Nation." Moreover, the "path it has taken to reach its outcome will, I fear, do damage to this institution."

Stevens vigorously objected to the maneuvering by the majority to review McCain-Feingold on its face and to overrule precedents, points not raised by the parties in the case. "Essentially, five Justices were unhappy with the limited nature of the case before us, so they changed the case to give themselves an opportunity to change the law." (That blunt assertion—a serious charge of unprincipled judging to serve an agenda—accords with Justice Kagan's accusation in *Janus* [chapter 2] that the majority justices were "weaponizing" the First Amendment.)

As for the majority's statement that a broad ruling was necessary because anything less would chill too much protected speech, Stevens said this concept rests on the unsubstantiated assumption that some "significant number of corporations have been cowed into quiescence by FEC 'censorship,'" an assumption that "is hard to square with practical experience." Stevens also disagreed with the majority's bypassing narrower ways to resolve the case "without toppling statutes and precedents." There were "principled, narrower paths that a court that was serious about judicial restraint could have taken" (a dart aimed directly at Chief Justice Roberts). As for stare decisis, "The only relevant thing that has changed since *Austin* . . . is the composition of this Court." The majority's ruling "strikes at the vitals of *stare decisis*," a doctrine that assures the people that "bedrock principles are founded in the law rather than in the proclivities of individuals."

Tweaking the nose of Justice Scalia and the originalists—those who believe the Constitution should be interpreted the way the original framers would have understood it—Stevens devoted an entire section of his opinion to "Original Understandings." Noting the eighteenth-century fears of "soulless" business corporations, Stevens quoted Thomas Jefferson's "hope" to "crush . . . the aristocracy of our monied corporations which dare already to challenge our government to a trial of strength and bid defiance to the laws of our country." Stevens asserted that when the framers wrote the First Amendment, "it was the free speech of individual Americans they had in mind," and they "took it as a given that corporations could be comprehensively regulated in the service of the public welfare."

As for more recent history, Stevens pointed out that Congress had placed limits on corporate campaign spending for more than a century, since 1907, after President Theodore Roosevelt declared to Congress that "all contributions by corporations to any political committee or for any political purpose should be forbidden by law."[12]

Stevens emphasized that corporations are different from individual speakers and should not be treated identically to natural persons. After all, unlike natural persons, corporations have certain characteristics, including limited liability, perpetual life, and favorable tax treatment for the accumulation of assets. They have "no consciences, no beliefs, no feelings, no thoughts, no desires. . . . [T]hey are not themselves members of 'We the People,' by whom and for whom our Constitution was established."

Stevens strongly disagreed with the majority's conclusion that independent expenditures could not corrupt or create the appearance of corruption. Combing through evidence about

Justice John Paul Stevens.

the realities of campaign finance, he demonstrated that independent expenditures can be even more corrupting than direct contributions. He argued, using real-world examples, that corporations can easily acquire "undue influence" over politicians both by making independent expenditures and by threatening to withhold them and support an opponent.

Fearing that as a result of the court's "blinkered and aphoristic approach to the First Amendment," a flood of corporate money would further distort and corrupt American political life, Stevens said. "Americans may be forgiven if they do not feel the court has advanced the cause of self-government today."

In conclusion, Stevens said, "Today's decision is backwards in many senses. It elevates the majority's agenda over the litigants' submissions, facial attacks over as-applied claims, broad constitutional theories over narrow statutory grounds, . . . assertion over tradition, absolutism over empiricism, rhetoric over reality. . . . While American democracy is imperfect, few outside the majority of this Court would have thought its flaws included a dearth of money in politics."

* * *

Stung by the part of Justice Stevens's dissent arguing that the majority's decision was not supported by the "original understanding" of the First Amendment, Justice Scalia filed a concurring opinion addressed to this issue, trying to rehabilitate originalism. His opinion was joined by Justice Thomas, the other avowed originalist on the court, and by Justice Alito.

Scalia noted that the text of the First Amendment makes no distinction between types of speakers,[13] and complained that the dissent found not "even an isolated statement from the founding era to the effect that corporations are *not* covered." Scalia acknowledged that statesmen from the founding

Justice Antonin Scalia.

era distrusted corporations, but said, "Most of the Founders' resentment towards corporations was directed at the state-granted monopoly privileges" that corporations then enjoyed. "Modern corporations do not have such privileges, and would probably have been favored by most of our enterprising Founders—excluding, perhaps, Thomas Jefferson and others favoring perpetuation of an agrarian society."

Scalia's "principal point" was "the conformity of today's opinion with the original meaning of the First Amendment. The Amendment is written in terms of 'speech,' not speakers."

In a final, triumphant pro-corporate flourish, Scalia concluded that "to exclude or impede corporate speech is to muzzle the principal agents of the modern free economy. We should celebrate rather than condemn the addition of this speech to the public debate."

The quarrel between Scalia and Stevens over the framers' understanding was inconclusive. Neither side could point to contemporaneous statements or specific historical evidence demonstrating the framers' actual intent. Apparently, we will never know what the framers had in mind, though it seems highly unlikely that the framers wanted the corporations they distrusted to have the same speech rights as individuals.

What *Citizens United* Did Not Do

Due to the complexities of campaign finance and its regulation, and the length and murkiness of the Kennedy opinion, the *Citizens United* decision has been widely misunderstood and blamed for some things the decision did *not* do. Here are the common ones:

Invent Corporate "Personhood"

The decision did not invent the concept of corporate "personhood" for constitutional purposes. Corporations have long been considered "legal persons" that could own property, make contracts, and sue and be sued. Treating them as persons with constitutional rights came in 1886, and the concept crept into our law by a fluke.

The Southern Pacific Railroad challenged a local property tax, and one of its arguments was that the tax deprived the railroad of "equal protection" of the law under the Fourteenth Amendment.[14] The Equal Protection Clause bars states from denying any "person" the equal protection of the law. When the case came before the Supreme Court for argument, Chief Justice Morrison Waite announced that the justices did not wish to hear argument on whether the amendment includes corporations as persons; "we are all of the opinion that it does." The court proceeded to rule that the railroad did not have to pay the tax, but did not make any ruling on the constitutional issue. The court did not address, analyze, or discuss the nature of corporations. Nor did it look to the language and purpose of the Fourteenth Amendment, which should have been the starting—and ending—point. The amendment's purpose was to ensure citizenship and legal protections for formerly enslaved persons. The amendment used the word "person" five times. It clearly referred only to natural persons in three instances, and there is no reason for a different meaning of the same word in the Equal Protection Clause. The court nevertheless treated the issue as resolved in favor of corporations.

However, there are many other mentions of "persons" in various other provisions of the Constitution, and they unmistakably refer to human beings, not corporations.[15] Also, the court has repeatedly ruled that a corporation is not a "person" within the meaning of the Fifth Amendment privilege against self-incrimination. But the court has never revisited the *Southern Pacific* ruling; nor has it heard argument or written a reasoned opinion on corporate personhood for constitutional purposes. Given *Bellotti, Citizens United,* and the twenty-four precedents cited in Justice Kennedy's opinion, it would now be hard to roll back the clock and determine that corporations (including, e.g., The New York Times Company, CBS News, et al.) have no First Amendment rights and can be censored at will. But intellectual honesty might at least have prompted the court to acknowledge that corporate personhood for constitutional purposes stands on a doctrinally and historically flimsy foundation.

Say "Money Is Speech"

As noted above, the court did not use this phrase at all. The closest it came was in quoting from *Buckley v. Valeo* to the effect that restricting campaign spending restricts the quantity of speech. That is self-evident: it costs money to print flyers and posters and to buy radio and television ads and billboard space. In a later case, discussed below, Chief Justice Roberts repeatedly treated cash as speech and, although the court did not use the exact words "money is speech," that is a fair, if informal, interpretation of the court's campaign finance jurisprudence.

When *Buckley* was decided, the great Harvard law professor Paul Freund said, "They say that money talks. I thought that was the problem, not the solution."[16]

Approve Super PACs

The court never mentioned super PACs. That is because super PACs did not exist. The creation of super PACs was probably an unintended consequence of the *Citizens United* decision. In writing the opinion, Justice Kennedy may not have imagined that super PACs would spring up to dominate campaign spending and dwarf the amounts directly contributed to candidates. But his reasoning led promptly and directly to the super PAC phenomenon.

Within weeks after the decision came down, the District of Columbia Court of Appeals decided that—as *Citizens United* instructed—a law limiting contributions to a conservative organization whose sole purpose was making independent expenditures violated the First Amendment.[17] Weeks later, the FEC issued an opinion allowing a liberal independent expenditures-only organization to accept unlimited contributions from corporations and unions.[18] In other words, contributions to independent expenditures organizations cannot be limited, and corporations can make them. Thus super PACs were launched. They exist mainly to make independent expenditures. They are a major player in many elections.

Give Wealthy Individuals and Corporations the Right to Make Unlimited Contributions to Politicians

The key word here is "contributions." *Citizens United* did not rule on the laws limiting direct contributions to a campaign and banning corporate contributions, and those laws remain in effect. Under the *Buckley* ruling, limits on contributions are constitutional, and corporations cannot contribute directly to candidates' campaigns. But corporations, unions, individuals, and now super PACs can spend independently, as much as they wish, as long as they do not coordinate with a candidate's campaign.

Authorize Billionaires and Corporations to Put "Dark Money" into Campaigns Secretly

To the contrary, *Citizens United* upheld the provisions of the McCain-Feingold law requiring the *disclosure* of funders of electioneering communications. By an 8–1 vote (Justice Thomas dissenting), the court rejected the contention that compelled disclosure would subject donors to harassment, thereby punishing their speech and violating their First Amendment rights.

The real loophole is Section 501(c)(4) of the Internal Revenue Code governing "social welfare" advocacy organizations like the US Chamber of Commerce and Karl Rove's Crossroads GPS. These groups are not supposed to be involved in supporting or opposing candidates (as opposed to advocating policy positions). But they in fact spend on elections. No donor disclosure is required. And there are no limits on the contributions to these organizations. Any billionaire or corporation that wants anonymity will find this dark money option attractive. This loophole preceded *Citizens United* and was not involved in the case at all. Section 501(c)(4) is an equal opportunity loophole, and liberal organizations as well as conservative ones use it. Perhaps because of *Citizens United*'s encouragement of election spending, shoveling money into 501(c)(4) organizations has become more popular.

Allow Foreign Corporations and Individuals to Spend on Campaigns

This was President Obama's misunderstanding. In his State of the Union speech days after the *Citizens United* decision, Obama criticized the justices' ruling, saying, "The Supreme Court reversed a century of law that I believe will open the floodgates for special interests—including foreign corporations—to spend without limit in our elections. I don't think American elections should be bankrolled by America's most powerful interests, or worse, by foreign entities." Several justices were seated just a few feet in front of the president, and television cameras caught Justice Alito mouthing the words "Not true."[19]

Obama was right about the floodgates, but Alito was right about foreign contributions and spending. The campaign finance law prohibits such foreign activity. Justice Kennedy's majority opinion expressly said, "We do not reach the question whether the Government has a compelling interest in preventing foreign individuals or associations from influencing our Nation's political process." In other words, the court simply left open the foreign spending issue. Any ruling against foreign spending would test the *Citizens United–Bellotti* principle that the First Amendment protects speech regardless of the identity of the speaker.

The Aftermath, and Near-Death, of Campaign Finance Reform

Not only did the *Citizens United* decision provide the rationale for and spark the creation of super PACs, but soon after the decision, the court decided three more campaign finance cases, building on and extending its rationale.

First, the court summarily—without hearing argument—threw out a long-standing Montana law restricting corporate spending in elections.[20] This was an exceptionally rude way to treat a state's democratically enacted law, a law based on Montana's unique history. Almost from the beginning of statehood, Montana's government had been bought and paid for by mining and other corporate interests. Its history demonstrated that corporations in fact engaged in quid pro quo corruption. But its law also prohibited independent expenditures.

The court, 5–4, disregarded the state's unusual history and peremptorily reversed the Montana Supreme Court's decision upholding the law. The majority merely cited *Citizens United* and effectively said, "We mean it!" Justice Breyer, joined by the other three more-liberal justices, dissented. He called attention to the state's unique history and to developments occurring since *Citizens United* such as the super PAC phenomenon. He also argued, citing Justice Stevens's dissent in *Citizens United,* that technically independent expenditures can be as corrupting as direct quid pro quo contributions and rejected the majority's "supposition that independent expenditures do not corrupt or appear to do so."

Second, the court invalidated Arizona's public finance alternative for campaign financing.[21] It was a matching scheme under which the state would make up the difference between the amount raised by a candidate accepting only public funds and any greater amount raised by a privately financed candi-

Justice Stephen Breyer.

date. At the oral argument in the Supreme Court, Chief Justice Roberts asked the state's lawyer whether the purpose of the law was not to level the playing field (a purpose condemned in *Citizens United*). When the lawyer said no, Roberts surprised him by saying he had "checked the [state's] web site this morning" and it said the purpose was to level the playing field.

The chief justice's opinion for the 5–4 majority held that the Arizona law impermissibly "burdened" political speech.

Roberts repeatedly treated cash as speech. For example, he said that, under the matching scheme, the state would give money in "direct response to the campaign speech" of an opponent. But what triggered the state's contribution was not what the opponent said but how much money had been raised.

Justice Kagan's dissent reasoned that the Arizona law did not restrict speech at all. It did not prohibit or limit what could be said; in fact, by providing an underfinanced candidate with matching funds, it provided for "more speech"—historically a First Amendment goal.

Third, the court threw out the federal law limiting the aggregate amount of contributions a person could make to candidates for Congress.[22] The case did not involve corporations. The would-be donor was a wealthy Alabama conservative businessman, Shaun McCutcheon, who wanted to contribute directly to the campaigns of a large number of candidates. He wanted to contribute the maximum allowed for each candidate, but that would exceed the aggregate limit.

In another opinion by Chief Justice Roberts, the court invalidated the aggregate limit. Roberts reasoned that the law was not narrowly tailored to preventing corruption, again using *Citizen United's* extremely limited concept of corruption. (Justice Thomas would have gone further and overruled *Buckley's* ruling that contribution limits did not violate the First Amendment, thus eliminating all campaign finance restrictions.) Justice Breyer's dissent objected to the court's unrealistically cramped view of the government's interest in maintaining contribution restrictions. He concluded that the court's reasoning "undermines, perhaps devastates, what remains of campaign finance reform."

And an Aberration

In 2015, just when it appeared that Chief Justice Roberts would never uphold a restriction on campaign finance, he wrote the opinion in *Williams-Yulee v. The Florida Bar*.[23] The case involved a candidate for a judgeship in Florida, a state in which judges are elected. Lanelle Williams-Yulee set up a website asking for public support as well as donations to her campaign. She also sent out a similar mass mailing. The Florida Bar charged her with violating its rule that prohibited candidates in judicial elections from personally soliciting campaign funds. The bar allowed candidates to form campaign committees who could solicit contributions, and candidates could speak at committee fundraisers as well as send thank-you notes to donors. But the bar contended its rule against personal solicitation was needed to protect "the integrity of the judiciary" and to maintain "the public's confidence in an impartial judiciary." It did not matter whether the persons solicited had any business that could come before the judge.

Roberts upheld the Florida Bar's rule. Not only was *Williams-Yulee* his only opinion upholding a campaign finance restriction, but it was only the second time in his entire tenure in which, in a 5–4 decision, he sided with the court's "liberals." (The other was his peculiar opinion in the Affordable Health Care Act case, saving Obamacare by finding that its individual mandate was not unconstitutional because it was a "tax.").[24] Perhaps he had an eye on his legacy and did not want history to record that he was completely close-minded on campaign finance cases.

Roberts began his opinion by declaring that "judges are not politicians, even when they come to the bench by way of the ballot." Judges, he asserted, should be treated differently from ordinary politicians. Roberts recognized that the Florida rule restricted political speech because of its content. Therefore, consistent with *Citizens United* and many other precedents, the court would have to exercise "strict scrutiny" of the state's justifications for the rule. He realized it is "rare" for a restriction to survive such scrutiny. But then he proceeded to find Florida's very general interests to be "compelling" and the no-personal-solicitation rule to be sufficiently narrowly tailored to serve those interests.

The Chief Justice's opinion substantially watered down strict scrutiny principles. He acknowledged that the Florida rule allowed a candidate to use a campaign committee for fundraisers and that it did not prohibit asking a lawyer, even one with a case before the judge, for a personal loan or for access to the lawyer's luxury box at a football stadium. He said the rule's "underinclusivity raises a red flag." (That is, if a law does not touch speech that is equally or more dangerous to the state's interests, this underinclusivity means the law is not narrowly tailored.) But "a state need not address all aspects of a problem in one fell swoop" and can "focus on [the] most pressing concerns." Personal requests for money would be "most likely to undermine public confidence in the integrity of the judiciary."

Roberts also rejected Williams-Yulee's argument that there was no good reason for Florida to prohibit her website and mass mailing requests for donations. She said these communications to a broad audience, rather than one on one, would not cause anyone to lose confidence in the judiciary. Roberts dismissed this contention by saying Florida reasonably determined that any personal appeal for money "inherently create[s] an appearance of impropriety that may cause the public to lose confidence in the integrity of the judiciary." (Recall that *Citizens United* did not exhibit any concern that independent expenditures would cause the public to lose confidence in the integrity of elected politicians.)

Justices Ginsburg and Breyer concurred, but, consistent with their position in the other campaign finance cases, did not agree that strict scrutiny was required.

The chief justice's conservative colleagues bitterly dissented. Justice Alito said the Florida rule "is about as narrowly tailored as a burlap bag." He said under the forgiving Roberts analysis, "narrow tailoring has no meaning, and strict scrutiny, which is essential to the protection of free speech, is seriously impaired." Justice Scalia excoriated the Chief's opinion, saying it was only "the appearance of strict scrutiny." Roberts's unsupported assertion that all personal solicitations "create a public appearance that undermines confidence in the judiciary" is not "strict scrutiny; it is sleight of hand." Scalia caustically suggested Roberts was not dispassionately applying First Amendment precedents but revealing an elitist view that it is undignified for judges to run for election and beg for money.

While the Roberts opinion was superficial and diluted First Amendment principles, the outcome of the case is not troubling: judges in states that elect judges and have rules like Florida's will not be able to solicit money. They may indeed be relieved not to have to grovel for money like ordinary politicians. What is troubling: *Citizens United* insists that *any* campaign finance restriction is constitutionally suspect and subject to strict scrutiny; this means that upholding a campaign finance limitation requires torturing First Amendment analysis, as Roberts did in *Williams-Yulee*.

Efforts to Change the *Citizens United* Ruling

Because *Citizens United* was a constitutional decision, neither Congress nor any state legislature can pass a law to change it.

That, however, did not discourage the city of Berkeley, California. On the city's 2014 ballot,[25] Proposition P asked the voters if the US Constitution should be amended "to abolish the concept that corporations are persons that are entitled to constitutional rights, and the doctrine that the expenditure of money may be treated as speech." The proposition garnered an amazing 85 percent of the vote. (Not one cent was spent on the Proposition P campaign, on either side.)

On the 2016 California ballot, a similar measure, Proposition 59,[26] appeared, instructing state officials to use all their authority to propose and ratify a constitutional amendment to overturn *Citizens United*, allow regulation or limitation of campaign contributions and spending, and "make clear that corporations should not have the same constitutional rights as human beings." Proposition 59 handily passed, prevailing over arguments that it was futile and that the First Amendment should not be tinkered with.

These quixotic efforts, and the fact that the great majority of Americans disapprove of *Citizens United*,[27] raise the question of whether anything can be done to reverse it or trim it back. Several constitutional amendments have been proposed—and gone nowhere. Senator Bernie Sanders was quick to propose one. It would have denied any constitutional rights to for-profit corporations. Others sought to undo corporate personhood altogether. None thought through the mischief that would be caused by removing First Amendment protection from media corporations like The New York Times Company and thereby allowing the government to censor them at will. (Invoking the Press Clause of the First Amendment is no answer, because the court has rejected—including in *Citizens United* itself—the contention that it gives whoever claims to be the "press" [a difficult definitional question in these days of *Fox News*, Twitter, and bloggers] speech rights not enjoyed by ordinary citizens.)

A possibly better amendment (it would be the twenty-eighth) would simply say something like: "Nothing in this constitution shall prevent Congress or any state from reasonably regulating and limiting contributions and expenditures relating to elections." The point is to allow reasonable control of spending in elections regardless of the sources or the mechanisms.

Legislation would be useful in containing the pernicious dark money influence on elections. The "DISCLOSE Act" was introduced in Congress; it would have required much more comprehensive, detailed, and timely disclosure of election spending, including independent expenditures. Real-time transparency, reporting online the top funders' spending, would at least alert voters to the interests backing a candidates. The act, like the constitutional amendments, has gone nowhere.

The Securities and Exchange Commission (SEC) could require publicly traded companies to disclose all their political spending. But the SEC has shown no inclination to do so. The Internal Revenue Service (IRS) could crack down on the abuses of 501(c)(4) organizations secretly amassing unlimited contributions and spending on elections. The underfunded and understaffed IRS, assuming it had the political will to act, will not do so.

State legislatures could enact new laws regulating companies incorporated in their states, perhaps requiring prior shareholder approval or denying tax deductions for political spending. They could also require the kinds of disclosures proposed by the DISCLOSE Act.

Until the 2016 election, one option for undoing *Citizens United* was replacing a conservative justice with a new appointee and hoping that a new majority might do to *Citizens United* what the Kennedy opinion did to *Austin*—overrule it. During the campaign, both Hillary Clinton and Bernie Sanders pledged to appoint only justices who would vote to overrule *Citizens United*. (Donald Trump did the same regarding *Roe v. Wade*.)

No one can know whether Merrick Garland, whom President Obama nominated when Justice Scalia died but who was denied even a hearing by the Republican leaders of the Senate, would have been inclined to abandon *Citizens United.* That possibility became moot when Trump won the electoral college. And his appointment of Neil Gorsuch and Brett Kavanaugh probably put off any reconsideration of *Citizens United* for decades. In the meantime, it is likely there will be more conservative attempts to stretch *Citizens United* to invalidate limits on contributions, prohibitions of direct corporate donations to campaigns and political parties, and other ways to maximize the influence of money on elections.

Lofty First Amendment Principles Obscure the Real Agenda

Justice Kennedy's opinion recited and reaffirmed several bedrock free speech tenets. He reminded everyone that "Speech is an essential mechanism for democracy, for it is the means to hold officials accountable to the people." He said the amendment "has its fullest and most urgent application to speech uttered during a campaign for public office." He reiterated that, when government is concerned about subversive, erroneous speech, "more speech, not less, is the governing rule," and he quoted the great Justice Louis Brandeis to the effect that "the remedy to be applied is more speech, not enforced silence." His focus on protecting speech regardless of the identity of the speaker was "premised on a mistrust of government power."

The court harnessed all this First Amendment energy in the service of corporate interests and those of the wealthy and powerful. Rather than helping the dispossessed and dissidents who need the amendment to get their voices heard and the lonely individuals who invoke the amendment to challenge en-

UNION DUES TALK, TOO

"Compelled Speech" as a Union-Busting Tactic

Citizens United was not the only case in which the Roberts Court, 5–4, treated the payment of money as speech, orchestrated an opportunity for a broad ruling, and overruled a decades-old precedent to achieve its desired result: a significant boost for politically conservative interests and a big loss for their traditional adversaries.

In *Janus v. American Federation of State, County, and Municipal Employees,*[1] the court inflicted a substantial wound on the political muscle of public employee unions. These are the unions that represent teachers, firefighters, and service workers, among others. The court ruled that employees who do not join the union cannot be charged anything to support the union's nonpolitical collective bargaining and other activities. This was a decision calculated to reduce financial support for unions and, therefore, the political support they have traditionally provided for liberal candidates and policies.

Unions are required to represent all employees in a bargaining unit, including those who choose not to become members of the union and do not pay dues. In a case called *Abood v. Detroit Board of Education,*[2] decided in 1977, the court determined that public sector unions (teachers, in that case) could not charge nonmembers for political activities (e.g., lobbying, supporting candidates). That decision protected the nonmembers' asserted First Amendment rights not to have to pay for "speech" by the unions they disagreed with.

However, under *Abood,* the unions were allowed to charge nonmembers a percentage of union dues—their "fair share"— reflecting the costs of collective bargaining and maintaining grievance systems. These are called "agency fees." Charging agency fees prevented workers who refused to pay dues from being "free riders," benefitting from routine union representation without paying for it. The *Abood* system was a compromise that accommodated two interests. It relieved nonmembers from having to subsidize political activities they did not agree with, yet it required them to contribute their fair share to the union's nonpolitical services on behalf of all the workers.

The system seemed to work just fine. Agency fees were used in twenty-two states. Over the years, as unions in the private sector lost members—and political power—public employee unions, such as teachers unions, became the voice of the labor movement. Unions now represent more than a third of public sector workers. And, because they provide substantial support for Democratic Party candidates and liberal policies, politically conservative forces stepped up to try to disempower the public unions. Their most effective tool, it turned out, was the First Amendment.

The National Right to Work Legal Defense Foundation brought a series of cases attacking the *Abood* precedent. In its fundraising for the litigation, Senator Rand Paul lauded the foundation's campaign as an "all-out assault on public sector forced unionism."[3] *Janus,* the case pending before the Supreme Court, had "the potential to remake the political landscape." Seeking tax-deductible contributions for the effort, Senator Paul said, "Even Big Labor attorneys themselves are admitting" the case "may well be life or death" for the unions.

In a 2012 case brought by the foundation to challenge agency fees, Justice Samuel Alito authored an opinion openly questioning whether *Abood* was correctly decided.[4] The court ended up ruling narrowly and not overturning *Abood*, but Alito virtually invited the filing of a case urging the court to abandon *Abood*. In 2014, the court dealt with another attack on agency fees, but because the workers were not full-time government employees, the court did not confront *Abood* head on.[5] Once again, Justice Alito wrote a menacing opinion that excoriated *Abood*. (Interestingly, much of his critique followed the reasoning of none other than Lewis Powell, who had written an opinion in *Abood*, disagreeing with the majority's rationale.[6])

Then the court finally found a case Alito and his conservative peers thought would be the vehicle for overruling *Abood*. It was a teachers-union case from California, in which teachers who did not belong to the union and who disagreed with the union's politics complained that their First Amendment rights were infringed because having to pay "fair share" agency fees amounted to "compelled speech."

When the court heard oral argument in the California case on January 11, 2016, it was obvious from the justices' remarks and questioning that the court would rule against the public unions. Indeed, in their deliberations after the argument, the justices voted 5–4 in favor of the dissident teachers, and Chief Justice Roberts assigned Justice Alito to write the majority opinion. Before the opinion could be filed, Justice Antonin Scalia unexpectedly died on February 13. That left the court deadlocked 4–4. In cases in which the court is evenly split, there can be no decision and, as a result, the ruling of the court below—in this case, the Court of Appeals for the Ninth Circuit—stands.[7] So public unions breathed a sigh of relief.

The relief did not last long. The *Janus* case had been percolating up toward the court. It had been initiated by the

Republican governor of Illinois, Bruce Rauner, whose campaign opposed organized labor. But a lower court found he lacked standing to raise the arguments of the state workers and dismissed the case; oddly, the court then allowed some actual workers (Mark Janus and two others) to intervene in the suit.[8] Despite these procedural irregularities, the case made its way, with the workers represented by the Right to Work Foundation, to the Supreme Court's docket.

President Obama had nominated Merrick Garland to replace Justice Scalia. Senate Republicans refused to give the moderate and highly qualified court of appeals judge a hearing. With the 2016 election, the Garland nomination lapsed, and Donald Trump promptly nominated Neil Gorsuch, who took his seat on the court on April 10, 2017. The court granted certiorari (agreed to hear the case) on September 28. A full complement of politically conservative justices was ready to bury *Abood*.

And that's what the *Janus* arguments and the opinions were mainly about: whether the doctrine of stare decisis (requiring courts to follow precedent) was a barrier to the court's desired result. Justice Alito brusquely decreed that requiring public employees to "subsidize" a union if they disagree with its positions "violates the free speech rights of nonmembers." This is so even if the objectors are charged only for nonpolitical services rendered. He particularly emphasized that "compelling individuals to mouth support for views they find objectionable" was unconstitutional and that compelling a person to subsidize the speech of others raised "similar" First Amendment concerns. (Paying for nonpolitical services rendered, however, is a far cry from being compelled to "mouth support for views" individuals do not believe in.)

Alito paid scant attention to whether being required to reimburse a union through a percentage of dues paid by members, for activities on behalf of all employees, was "speech" within the meaning of the First Amendment. The nonmembers were not required to say anything or refrain from saying anything. Indeed, there is a well-founded argument that "being forced to pay money to objectionable causes is a fact of life, not a First Amendment problem."[9] Of course, the amendment protects the speech of dissidents in general, but that does not mean being required to reimburse a union for nonpolitical services rendered is "compelled speech."

The bulk of Alito's opinion was devoted to whether *Abood* should be overruled. Acknowledging "the importance of following precedent unless there are strong reasons for not doing so," he said *Abood* was "poorly reasoned," led to "practical problems," and was inconsistent with "more recent decisions" (his own opinions in the cases leading up to *Janus*). Nor was there sufficient real-world "reliance" on the agency fee arrangements set up by *Abood* "to justify the perpetuation of the free speech violations that *Abood* has countenanced for the past 41 years. *Abood* is therefore overruled." An echo of *Citizens United.*

But unlike in *Citizens United*, the majority could not plead ignorance of the real-world consequences of its decision. Alito was fairly blunt about the *Janus* decision's likely impact on the ability of public unions to survive economically without the support of all employees and on their ability, therefore, to act in the political arena. Alito said, "We recognize that the loss of payments from nonmembers may cause unions to experience unpleasant transaction costs" and may lose members. "But we must weigh these disadvantages against the considerable windfall that unions have received under *Abood* for the past 41 years. It is hard to estimate how many billions of dollars have been taken from nonmembers and transferred to public-sector unions in violation of the First Amendment. Those unconstitutional exactions cannot be allowed to continue indefinitely."[10] Court to left-leaning unions: Take that!

Justice Elena Kagan wrote an impassioned dissent. She objected to the majority's "six-year campaign to reverse *Abood.*" She contended that the *Abood* compromise had worked admirably well for governments in managing their employees and workplaces. The decision "has proved workable," and is "deeply entrenched, in both the law and the real world." Judicial disruption of reliance on the *Abood* system was indefensible. Justice Kagan spent most of her opinion rebutting Alito's assertions on why respect for precedent did not bar overruling *Abood.*

On the merits, Kagan pointed out that the court had often upheld schemes under which mandatory dues for organizations that "speak" were held not to present any First Amendment problems. For example, the court had approved imposing fees on state bar members for professional expression,[11] on university students to subsidize campus events,[12] and on fruit processors for generic advertising.[13] These situations are not unlike taxpayers having to subsidize governments whose positions they may abhor, which does not present any First Amendment problem.[14]

(Justice Kagan might have added that the majority's solicitude for protecting dissident workers from union speech they opposed was in sharp contrast to the *Citizens United* court's dismissive treatment of dissident shareholders who object to corporate speech. In *Citizens United* the majority was willing to rely on "corporate democracy" to protect dissident shareholders whose money was devoted to political causes they disagreed with, but in *Janus* it was not willing to rely on "union democracy" to protect dissident workers; instead, it upset the entire system by decreeing that helping to defray the union's costs was "compelled speech.")

It was in *Janus* that Justice Kagan accused the conservative majority of "weaponizing the First Amendment, in a way

Justice Elena Kagan and Chief Justice Roberts.

that unleashes judges, now and in the future, to intervene in economic and regulatory policy." She said the majority had improperly seized the opportunity to determine the winners of the debate over whether agency fees arrangements were good policy. (There were twenty-two states on one side of the debate, allowing agency fees, and twenty-eight on the other). "Most alarming, the majority has chosen the winners by turning the First Amendment into a sword, and using it against workaday economic and regulatory policy." Because "speech is everywhere," almost all economic and regulatory policy "affects or touches speech. So, the majority's road runs long. And at every stop are black-robed rulers[15] overriding citizens' choices. The First Amendment was meant for better things."

Janus was the last decision in the first century of Supreme Court free speech cases. The First Amendment used to be meant for better things. Now the black-robed rulers are armed with expansive notions of what "speech" is, and with inflexible, doctrinaire First Amendment analysis. These weapons have the potential to usher in a new *Lochner* era, with the majority using the First Amendment rather than the Fourteenth to advance its own notions of proper economic regulation and strike down laws disfavored by conservative interests.

Indeed, not content with its *Janus* triumph, on December 4, 2018, the National Right to Work Foundation filed a petition asking the court to decide "Whether it violates the First Amendment to appoint a labor union to represent and speak for public-sector employees who have declined to join the union."[16] The First Amendment outright bans public employee unions? There will always be those urging the black-robed rulers to expand their domain.

3

A BUSINESS-FRIENDLY FIRST AMENDMENT

Curtailing Government Regulation in the Name of Free Speech

What does it mean to say the court is "business friendly"? It means the justices, especially the politically conservative majority, are receptive to petitions filed by corporations and business associations; they vote to hear and decide a large number of business cases while declining to hear hundreds of pleas from, for example, criminal defendants, workers, nonprofit organizations, and aggrieved ordinary citizens. It means the justices are sympathetic to arguments that government regulations interfere too much with business operations and profitability and that businesses need to be protected from lawsuits and liability. It means the justices decide cases favoring corporate and business interests over other societal interests such as consumer and environmental protection and the rights of injured individuals to receive fair compensation. It means the legal analysis the justices use in deciding cases makes it easier for business interests to prevail and harder for others to gain access to the courts to redress their grievances.

Many observers have noted how favorably American corporations and business interests have been treated by the Roberts Court. One said, referring to Lewis Powell's Chamber of Commerce memo, "the Roberts Court came to represent the apotheosis of Powell's vision."[1] Another, based on empirical studies, proclaimed that the Roberts Court "is the most pro-

business of any since the Second World War."[2] The five conservative justices rank in the top ten most business-friendly
justices of the last seventy years. When Chief Justice Roberts was in private practice, he was "the go-to lawyer for the
business community" and was hired by the US Chamber of
Commerce to represent it in at least two cases.[3] The majority
justices' affiliation with and support of the Federalist Society
(often giving speeches at society events), and their early lawyer-
ing experience in the Reagan Administration, reinforced their
willingness to credit business contentions that government
regulations were unduly burdensome.

It comes as no surprise, therefore, that the Roberts Court
has elected to accept cases that involve business interests, to
decide cases favoring such interests and to decide them in ways
that serve business interests for the foreseeable future. There
are too many of such cases to mention, but here's a sample of
some of them:

- The court held (5–4) in 2018 that employers could ex-
tract from employees (via a "contract" emailed to them) an
"agreement" that any disputes would be arbitrated and not
brought to a court.[4] The employees contended that they had
been underpaid in violation of the Fair Labor Standards Act.
Their claims were too small to be worth litigating individual-
ly, but the court upheld the boilerplate contract's "waiver" of
the right to bring a class action. The court rejected the argument that banding together in a class action was a "concerted
activity" protected by the National Labor Relations Act.

- In 2011, the court decided (5–4) that consumers who
were defrauded when they bought cell phones could not sue
because their contracts disallowed class actions and required
arbitration.[5] The court said state laws that prohibited such
contracts (as unconscionable because the buyers had no bar-

gaining power, damages were small, and there was a deliberate scheme to defraud) were "preempted" by federal law.

- In 2013, the court held (5–3, Justice Sotomayor not participating) that American Express could not be sued for antitrust violations because, by contract, its customers' claims of anticompetitive behavior had to be arbitrated.[6] Justice Kagan dissented, saying the company had "insulated itself from antitrust liability, even if it has in fact violated the law."

- In 2011, the court spared Wal-Mart, the country's largest employer, from having to defend a class action brought by women claiming sex discrimination in pay and promotions.[7]

- In 2007, in the famous Lily Ledbetter case, the court ruled (5–4) that a woman who had been employed for 20 years by Goodyear Tire & Rubber and underpaid the whole time could not win her sex discrimination case because she had not sued within 180 days of receiving a too-low paycheck.[8] Justice Ginsburg's eloquent dissent pointed out that Ledbetter was the lowest paid of sixteen managers and was the only woman, and that pay disparities are not as observable as refusals to hire or promote and are "often hidden from sight." It took an act of Congress to change the court's ruling.

- In 2015, regarding environmental interests, the court decided (5–4) that an Environmental Protection Agency (EPA) regulation of fossil-fueled power plants for emissions under the Clean Air Act was invalid.[9] Justice Kagan's dissent complained the majority was micromanaging how the agency took costs into consideration, and "the result is a decision that deprives the American public of the pollution control measures" that the EPA found "would save many, many lives."

- In 2013, the court ruled (5–4) against a woman who had been horribly disfigured and disabled by taking a defectively designed drug.[10] The court said her state law claim was "preempted" by federal law. Justice Alito wrote for the majority that the victim's "situation is tragic and evokes deep sympathy, but a straightforward application of preemption law requires that the judgment below be reversed." (How "straightforward" can it be when four Supreme Court justices vigorously disagree?)

The US Chamber of Commerce, remembering Justice Powell's cue, filed *amicus* briefs supporting the corporations' contentions in every one of these cases.

The First Amendment Becomes a Business-Friendly Tool

The Roberts Court's willingness to shield business interests from antitrust, consumer, employment, and environmental regulation carries over to the First Amendment arena, where the court has repeatedly invoked the amendment as an anti-regulatory device. Indeed, one keen observer concluded from an empirical study that "corporations increasingly displaced individuals as direct beneficiaries of First Amendment rights" and said that there has been a "corporate takeover of the First Amendment."[11]

Drug Marketing Data Is "Speech"?

As Exhibit A regarding the court's conversion of the First Amendment into a formidable weapon for corporations, consider *Sorrell v. IMS Health, Inc.*[12] Just as the *Janus* majority manipulated the definition of "speech" to cover the payment of money for services rendered, the majority in *Sorrell* manipulated the definition of "speech" to cover the purchase and sale of drug prescription data, information collected pursuant to regulatory mandate. Both decisions fit the *Lochner* pattern.

Vermont passed a law regulating commerce in doctors' drug prescription data. It prohibited the pharmacies that fill prescriptions from selling the doctors' data, without the consent of the doctors, to "data miners" who in turn sell the data to drug manufacturers. The manufacturers' salespeople would then use the data to sharpen their sales pitches to doctors in an attempt to get the doctors to prescribe their brand name drugs rather than generics. The Vermont law prohibited all such purchases and sales.

The state defended the law by claiming an interest in maintaining medical privacy and confidentiality, in avoiding potential harassment of doctors, in the integrity of the physician-patient relationship, and in holding down the price of drugs.

The Roberts Court, in a baffling and almost impenetrable opinion by Justice Anthony Kennedy, found the Vermont law an unconstitutional abridgment of free speech. The vote was 6–3, with Justice Sotomayor—without a word of explanation—joining the five politically conservative justices. (Seven years later, in *Janus*, the justice basically disavowed this vote, apparently after realizing what the court was doing with the First Amendment.) Justice Kennedy, as in *Citizens United* and in many other cases, was the Roberts Court's most bullish supporter of First Amendment freedoms. In *Sorrell*, Kennedy significantly expanded the speech rights of corporations.

Kennedy dismissively brushed off what should have been the key consideration in the case: whether the sale and use of the prescriber data is "speech" within the meaning of "the freedom of speech." Kennedy simply asserted that "speech in aid of pharmaceutical marketing . . . is a form of expression protected by the Free Speech Clause of the First Amendment."[13]

Having decreed that buying and selling the data would be treated as speech, Kennedy then announced that the law was subject to "heightened scrutiny" under the First Amendment. That was because the law singled out "marketing speech" for disfavored treatment based on its content, and it singled out the "speakers" (data miners and pharmaceutical manufacturers) for disfavored treatment: "The law on its face burdens disfavored speech by disfavored speakers." Kennedy added that the law was "aimed at a particular viewpoint": promotion of brand-name drugs. These considerations—discrimination based on content, speaker, and viewpoint—have some First Amendment pedigree, but had not been thought to apply to ordinary economic regulations.

The heightened scrutiny that Kennedy exercised required that Vermont, to save its regulation, prove that the law furthered a substantial state interest, that the law "directly advanced" that interest, and that it was "drawn to achieve that interest." Kennedy called this "intermediate" scrutiny. He basically pooh-poohed the state's interests as not very important and not really served by the data restriction. He also uncovered what he saw as a loophole, in that the law allowed pharmacies to disclose prescription data for academic research purposes, so the law did not prevent the evils the state claimed to be preventing. He concluded that the law did not hold up under scrutiny and therefore was unconstitutional.

The US Chamber of Commerce, in addition to various components of the pharmaceutical industry, filed *amicus curiae* briefs urging the court to do exactly what it did: condemn the law as a violation of the freedom of corporate speech.

Justice Breyer's Dissent

Justice Stephen Breyer is no First Amendment absolutist. He is reluctant to use categories like "content-based," "compelling interest," and "strict scrutiny" to resolve free speech issues. He favors more of a balancing act, allowing courts to determine whether speech restrictions "work harm to First Amendment interests that is disproportionate to their furtherance of legitimate regulatory objectives." In *Sorrell*, Breyer said the "regulatory actions of the kind present here have not previously been thought to raise serious" First Amendment concerns. Indeed, "until today, this Court has *never* found that the *First Amendment* prohibits the government from restricting the use of information pursuant to a regulatory mandate." (Pharmacies are required by federal law to collect prescriber data.) "Nor has this Court *ever* previously applied any form of 'heightened' scrutiny in any even roughly similar case."[14]

Breyer pointed out that "regulatory programs necessarily draw distinctions on the basis of content." For example, public utility regulators impose all sorts of restrictions on regulated companies, the Federal Reserve imposes restrictions on banks, and the Food and Drug Administration imposes strict regulations on what food and drug companies can say about their products. These regulations are aimed at specific speakers because only the regulated companies are subject to them. These regulations should not, in Breyer's view, be subject to "heightened" scrutiny, especially the unforgiving brand of scrutiny the court applied in *Sorrell*.

As for how the First Amendment should apply, Breyer reasoned that the Vermont law caused only "modest" harm to commercial interests (merely preventing the drug company salespeople from making more effective sales pitches), but invalidating the law caused substantial interference with the state's goals.

Drawing a direct parallel to the *Lochner* era, Breyer said the court's approach in *Sorrell* "threatens to return us to a happily bygone era when judges scrutinized legislation for its interference with economic liberty. History shows that the power was much abused and resulted in the constitutionalization of economic theories preferred by individual jurists. . . . Today's majority risks repeating the mistakes of the past." Breyer lamented that, "at best the Court opens a Pandora's Box of First Amendment challenges to many ordinary regulatory practices that may only incidentally affect a commercial message. At worst, it reawakens *Lochner's* pre–New Deal threat of substituting judicial for democratic decision-making where ordinary economic regulation is at issue." In other words, judges, using free speech rather than due process principles, will be free to overturn economic regulations at the behest of corporations claiming their "speech" is being abridged.

*   *   *

It is worth remembering the reasons why speech deserves constitutional protection. Historically, scholars, thinkers, courts, and well-informed citizens have recognized three main rationales for providing legal protection for free speech. First, the ascertainment of truth: it is more likely that the truth will emerge from challenging debate in the marketplace of ideas than if government decides what ideas are correct. Second, we need free speech in order to facilitate (and keep) a self-governing democracy, replacing bad officials with better ones and disastrous policies with effective ones. Third, freedom of speech permits autonomous individuals to express themselves as they wish and to become fuller human beings.

Occasionally, a fourth rationale is mentioned, a negative reason for protecting speech: we do not trust government to make sound decisions about what kind of speech is good or bad for us. It is this rationale that underpins some of the Roberts Court's First Amendment decisions, especially the pro-business ones.

None of these rationales is honored by the court's *Sorrell* decision. Striking down the Vermont statute did not enhance the search for truth in the marketplace of ideas. It actually disserved the interest in preserving a self-governing democracy. It certainly did nothing to enhance individual self-fulfillment. It was not necessary to prevent government from dictating what is acceptable speech. In short, throwing out the Vermont law did not serve any of the purposes for which we protect free speech. *Sorrell* should not have been a First Amendment case. It was simply an opportunity to deregulate business.

"Commercial Speech"

Before 1976, "commercial speech" had no First Amendment protection at all.[15] Advertising could be, and was, restricted by various laws in various jurisdictions. Then, with Lewis Powell still a justice, the court decided *Virginia State Board of Pharmacy v. Virginia Citizens Consumer Council.*[16] In a suit by consumer groups led by Ralph Nader, the court threw out a Virginia law that banned advertising the prices of prescription drugs. The court's decision did not turn on pharmacies' right, as speakers, to speak freely. Rather, the court reasoned that their audience—consumers —had a strong interest in obtaining useful information. The free flow of truthful information to the public implicated First Amendment concerns. Protection for commercial speech thus depended on the informing-the-public function, while traditional First Amendment doctrine—for instance, protection of soapbox iconoclasts—emphasized the rights of the speakers. In other words, the only good reason to invoke the First Amendment to protect commercial speech is to ensure that listeners are not deprived of information useful to them.

In decisions following *Virginia Pharmacy*, the court extended its reasoning to cover a wide variety of commercial speech, and now, as one scholar found in an empirical study, businesses are winning more free speech cases than individuals.[17] The test the court uses for commercial speech cases is similar to that used by Justice Kennedy in *Sorrell*, asking in part whether there is a good "fit" between the government's interest and the precise restriction. As Harvard's John Coates found, application of this test has substantially liberated commercial speakers. But "imperfectly fitting rules and statutes are part of the price of political compromise, which is the essence of the American method of lawmaking."[18] In other words, insisting on exacting scrutiny of commercial regulations is inconsistent with democratic rather than judicial governing. The court in *Sorrell* did not vindicate the expressive interests of any individual, but simply enhanced the ability of the pharmaceutical industry to make more money.

As Robert Post and Amanda Shanor have pointed out, cases like *Sorrell* have nothing to do with engaging in democratic self-determination—buying and selling prescription data is simply transacting business.[19] "Different kinds of speech embody different constitutional values, and each kind of speech should receive constitutional protections appropriate to the value it embodies." Traditional First Amendment principles prohibit content discrimination to allow people to participate in public debate regardless of what they have to say. But commercial speech should be protected only to the extent needed to serve the public need for useful information. "The principles that protect public discourse do not apply to commercial speech."

The conservatives on the Roberts Court have increasingly questioned why commercial speech should not have full First Amendment protection. Justice Thomas would simply abolish any distinction and give commercial speech the same protection as political speech.[20] While it may not be easy to distinguish one from the other in some cases, it is important to try.

Justice Clarence Thomas.

For example, there is no reason to tolerate false or misleading commercial speech (e.g., lies or baseless claims about products) but our free speech traditions—and landmark Supreme Court decisions—require us to tolerate false or misleading political speech (e.g., about one's credentials or opponents' positions). We depend for the correction of such erroneous political speech on the marketplace of ideas in the political arena, not government rules. As the Supreme Court remarked in *New York Times v. Sullivan*,[21] in holding that false and defamatory statements about public officials are not deprived of First Amendment protection, "debate on public issues should be uninhibited, robust, and wide-open, and . . . it may well include vehement, caustic, and sometimes unpleasantly sharp attacks on government and public officials." That principle does not apply to commercial speech.

In a stunning display of judicial activism, in a case in which no party raised the issue, Justice Thomas called for the court to "reconsider,"[22] and presumably overrule, *New York Times v. Sullivan*. The decision has been the law of the land since 1964. Seizing on an opportunity to air his originalist theory, he reconstructed history and concluded that *Sullivan* and the many cases following it were "policy-driven decisions masquerading as constitutional law." He saw no irony in condemning one of the great pillars of American free speech law while at the same time calling for greater protection for commercial speech, corporate spending on elections, and antiunion public employees—none of which would have been understood by the framers of the Constitution as favored by the Free Speech Clause. Fortunately, no other member of the Roberts Court has joined Thomas's opinion—yet.

Ominous Signs: Deploying a First Amendment Cannon to Shoot Down a Pipsqueak, Defenseless Adversary

To get the answers one wants, it helps to frame the questions. So it is with First Amendment adjudication in the Roberts Court. If the justices' preferred outcome is to favor corporate and conservative interests—finding them within the protection of "the freedom of speech"—the court must use an analytical framework that yields that result.

Over the first century of deciding free speech cases (starting with *Schenck v. United States* in 1919), the court developed various analytical frameworks—the questions that must be answered—for arriving at a reasoned decision. For example,

in recent decades the court has determined that if a law punishes or suppresses speech because of its message or content,
it is presumed unconstitutional, the court must exercise "strict
scrutiny" of the reasons said to support it, and the government must prove that the law serves a "compelling" interest
and is "narrowly tailored" to serve that interest. Therefore, the
questions that must be answered are whether the law really is
content based, how strong the government's interest is, and
whether there is a good fit ("narrow tailoring") between the
law's restrictions and the interest served.

The Roberts Court has used this analysis in many free
speech cases. It is a very demanding test. When the court exercises strict scrutiny, the speech restriction is almost always
found to violate the First Amendment. The court tends to accept the government's assertion that its interest is compelling,
but then to find a lack of narrow tailoring, often (but not always) determining that the restriction is overinclusive (banning
more speech than necessary to serve the interest) or underinclusive (leaving untouched similar speech that poses as much
or more danger to the government interest). The court has
often said the restriction must be the "least restrictive means"
of serving the interest. The court has sometimes said there
must be "evidence" the restriction is "actually necessary" to
solve some problem. The court has not been consistent in applying strict scrutiny, which it sometimes calls "exacting," "demanding," or "heightened." The point is that the way the court
frames the question usually dictates the answer.

In a very peculiar 2015 case, the court announced a new
wrinkle in its strict scrutiny analysis. It planted an antiregulatory seed in a hidden place, where it can sprout and serve as
a powerful weapon against nettlesome government regulation
of business. It was an easy and inconsequential case, but in
a stealthy move, the conservative majority laid out a revised

framework that threatens the constitutionality of many kinds of government economic and health regulations.

The case was *Reed v. Town of Gilbert.*[23] The Arizona town, like most municipalities, regulated what kinds of signs could be posted in public places. But Gilbert's sign ordinance was quite unusual. It differentiated among "political," "ideological," and "temporary directional" signs and treated them differently. Political signs ("Vote for Jones!") could be as large as 32 square feet and could stay in place during an entire election season. Ideological signs about general issues ("Abortion Is Murder!") could stay in place indefinitely but were limited to 20 square feet. Directional signs (like those announcing church services and other community events and telling people where to find them) were limited to 6 square feet and could be displayed only just before and after an event.

The Good News Community Church posted signs around town informing the public of the time and location of its services. The church was cited by a town compliance officer for not taking the signs down in time. Officials confiscated one sign. The church challenged the restriction on its signs on First Amendment grounds.

The Supreme Court decided the ordinance violated the First Amendment. The court's vote was unanimous, but its reasoning was not. Justice Clarence Thomas wrote the majority opinion. He cleverly ridiculed the ordinance, revealing its absurdity (though it was an easy target), saying it applied differently depending entirely on the "communicative content" of the sign:

> If a sign informs its reader of the time and place a book club will discuss John Locke's Two Treatises of Government, that sign will be treated differently from a sign expressing the view that one should vote for one of Locke's

followers in an upcoming election, and both signs will be treated differently from a sign expressing an ideological view rooted in Locke's theory of government. More to the point, the Church's signs inviting people to attend its worship services are treated differently from signs conveying other types of ideas.[24]

Justice Thomas's opinion concluded the ordinance was a content-based regulation and did not survive strict scrutiny. But it introduced a new element to the determination of when a law is content based. According to Thomas, "Government regulation of speech is content based if a law applies to particular speech *because of the topic discussed* or the idea or message expressed," citing the court's opaque opinion in the *Sorrell* pharmaceutical case. He said a speech regulation targeted at specific *subject matter* is content based "even if it does not discriminate among viewpoints within that subject matter." And such a law is subject to strict scrutiny "regardless of the government's benign motive, content-neutral justification, or lack of 'animus toward the ideas contained' in the regulated speech."[25]

Applying strict scrutiny, Thomas made short work of the town's justifications for the ordinance. He assumed preserving the town's aesthetic appeal and ensuring traffic safety were "compelling" reasons for regulating signs. But the distinctions among the categories of signs were irrational and arbitrary, almost nonsensical, so the ordinance was not narrowly tailored to serve those interests.

The Thomas opinion—its eagerness to find a law content based, its expansive notion of what makes a law content based, and its near-automatic condemnation of a law using strict scrutiny—is likely to cause First Amendment mischief. It is a template that can easily be used to invalidate many kinds of commercial regulations.[26]

Justices Breyer and Kagan both wrote separate opinions, concurring only in the outcome, not in Thomas's reasoning. As he did in *Sorrell*, Breyer rejected any mechanical approach to content discrimination and strict scrutiny. These concepts may be useful "rules of thumb," but should not be determinative. In his view, content discrimination "should not always trigger strict scrutiny," and strict scrutiny should not automatically result in invalidating a law. Instead, Breyer would ask "whether the regulation at issue works harm to First Amendment interests that is disproportionate in light of the relevant regulatory objectives." Breyer said, "Answering this question requires examining the seriousness of the harm to speech, the importance of the countervailing objectives, the extent to which the law will achieve those objectives, and whether there are other, less restrictive ways of doing so." This approach, Breyer asserted, would result in upholding more democratically enacted speech restrictions. That may be so, though Breyer's approach invites judges to make their own judgments about how valuable certain speech is and how important the government's interests are and to weigh whether the restriction is "disproportionate." Moreover, most of Breyer's listed considerations are supposed to be addressed in applying the familiar "narrow tailoring" part of strict scrutiny.

Justice Kagan's opinion, joined by Breyer and Justice Ginsburg, worried that "unless courts water down strict scrutiny," cities "will find themselves in an unenviable bind: They will have to either repeal the exemptions that allow for helpful signs on streets and sidewalks, or else lift their sign restrictions altogether and resign themselves to the resulting clutter."

Beyond trying to preserve useful municipal signage, Kagan addressed the broader issues. She would limit the use of strict scrutiny to cases in which it is necessary "to preserve an uninhibited marketplace of ideas in which truth will ultimately prevail," and "to ensure that the government has not regulated speech 'based on hostility—or favoritism—towards the underlying message expressed.' "[27] These are cases in which there is a "realistic possibility that official suppression of ideas is afoot." That is "always the case when the regulation facially differentiates on the basis of viewpoint," and almost always the case when a law restricts discussion of an entire topic.

Kagan would "administer our content-regulation with a dose of common sense," rather than invalidate laws that do not threaten core First Amendment concerns. Kagan nevertheless concurred in the *Reed* result because the town's distinctions did not pass "strict scrutiny, or intermediate scrutiny, or even the laugh test. . . . I see no reason why such an easy case calls for us to cast a constitutional pall on reasonable regulations quite unlike the law before us."

Nothing in the facts of *Reed* involved a threat to the ascertainment of truth in the marketplace of ideas, an attempt to suppress speech that the government disapproves, or a hindrance to individual self-fulfillment. In other words, the court's decision was not needed to serve the purposes for which we protect free speech. Rather, it was about reining in what the court viewed as unnecessary meddling by a local government, consistent with the Roberts Court's antiregulatory bent. Whether the Thomas expansion of the universe of content-based measures leads the court to ratchet up its review and condemnation of other common business regulations is worth worrying about. The analytical framework laid in *Reed* is ready to facilitate these new uses of the First Amendment.

BOWS TO THE RELIGIOUS RIGHT AND THE UNHOLY ALLIANCE OF BUSINESS AND RELIGION

For most of American history, all the justices of the Supreme Court were Protestant. Now, there are six Catholics and three Jews on the court. There is no obvious answer for how that happened. The religious imbalance raises the question of whether the justices' religious beliefs affect their decisions. The justices would certainly deny that. They would say they simply apply the law to the facts, umpire-like, without regard to their own religion.

Just as the Roberts Court has been friendly to corporations and business interests, it has been friendly to Christian right interests. For example, it has held that a town council can recite prayers at the beginning of every meeting,[1] a city can keep a Ten Commandments monument in a public park,[2] the federal government can keep a cross on federally managed land,[3] and none of these activities violates the Establishment Clause of the First Amendment. The court has denied the right of tax-payers to sue to challenge the Bush Administration's "faith-based initiatives"[4] as well as the right to sue over tax credits for parochial school tuition.[5] The court ruled that a Missouri state constitutional provision forbidding the use of taxpayer funds for churches (to fix up school playgrounds) violated the Free Exercise Clause.[6] None of these cases involved the Speech Clause. Many of these cases involved religious litigating organizations, such as the Alliance Defending Freedom and the Becket Fund for Religious Liberty.

Burwell v. Hobby Lobby[7] was probably the Roberts Court's most controversial decision favoring Christian right interests. It was not a First Amendment case. It was not even a constitutional case. But it vividly revealed the majority justices' mindset and their receptivity to accepting fundamentalist religious contentions.

Hobby Lobby Stores, Inc. is a for-profit corporation with more than 23,000 employees. Its owners, David and Barbara Green and their three children, are Evangelical Christians. They objected to the provision of the Affordable Care Act that required large employers to include contraception in their health insurance plans. The Greens believe that some forms of birth control cause abortion, and they oppose abortion on religious grounds. They had the Hobby Lobby corporation sue the federal government under the Religious Freedom Restoration Act, enacted in 1993, which provides for an exemption from federal laws imposing a substantial burden on "a person's exercise of religion."

In a 5–4 decision divided along familiar conservative-liberal lines, the court ruled the corporation could claim an exemption from the birth control requirement. Justice Samuel Alito wrote the opinion. He basically pierced the corporate veil, finding that the corporation had religious rights because its owners did. "A corporation is simply a form of organization used by human beings to achieve desired ends." Protecting the "free-exercise rights of corporations" like Hobby Lobby "protects the religious liberty of the humans who own and control those companies." (It also shields corporations from bothersome regulation.)

* * *

Exempting religionists from laws of general application they object to has become a major focus of the religious right and

Justice Samuel Alito.

the legal campaign brought by organizations like the Alliance Defending Freedom. The Roberts Court has been receptive to their claims. And just as business-friendly rulings have spilled over into the First Amendment arena, so too have rulings in religious right cases under the Speech Clause of the First Amendment. This is where the interests of business and the religious right coincide: invoking the First Amendment to avoid unwanted regulation.

The famous *Cakeshop* case in 2018 opened the door for businesses whose owners are religiously opposed to, for example, same-sex marriage, to claim exemption from anti-discrimination laws.[8] The case arose when a Colorado baker, Jack Phillips, refused to sell a wedding cake to a gay couple, citing his religious scruples against same-sex marriage. The Colorado Civil Rights Commission found this action violated the state's antidiscrimination law, which, like many others, provided that businesses could not deny service to people based on characteristics such as race, religion, sex, and sexual orientation. The law was a content-neutral regulation of businesses selling goods and services. But Phillips claimed that being required by the state to bake a cake for a gay couple violated both the free speech and the religious-exercise provisions of the First Amendment. The speech claim was that the state was "compelling" him to exercise his artistic talents to express a message with which he disagreed. He could not be required by government to "say" something that violated his religious beliefs.

The pendency of the case in the Supreme Court generated national debates over the rights of gay people, respect for same-sex marriage, the obligation to comply with neutral laws of general application, whether businesspeople can be required by government to compromise their religious scruples, and even whether baking a cake can be considered "speech" protected by the Free Speech Clause. All these issues were involved in the *Cakeshop* case. The court was flooded with at least ninety-five *amicus curiae* briefs arguing all sides of the issues.[9] Christian right demonstrators paraded in front of the Supreme Court building with signs demanding, for example, "End Abuse of Christians Now!"

The case seemingly would be a major event in the culture war, pitting religious fundamentalists who oppose same-sex marriage against gay and civil rights interests. As Justice Kennedy put it in his opinion for the 7–2 majority, the case required reconciling a state's "authority to protect the rights and dignity of gay persons who are, or wish to be, married but who face discrimination when they seek goods or services" with the "right of all persons" to exercise First Amendment freedoms.

The court ducked the free speech issue altogether. Instead, Justice Kennedy found a way to rule in the baker's favor without destroying the effectiveness of public accommodations

Pro-*Cakeshop* demonstrators at the Supreme Court.

laws or upsetting decades of civil rights precedents. Seizing on two obscure remarks by individual Colorado commissioners during the extensive state proceedings, Kennedy found that the commission had not considered the baker's case "with the religious neutrality that the Constitution requires." Phillips therefore prevailed on this procedural ground. (Kennedy's hypersensitive straining to find religious bias contrasts with his curt rejection of nonbelievers' claims in the town council prayers case four years earlier.[10])

It was obvious that a majority of the justices (including Kennedy) wanted to rule for Phillips, and a different majority (including Kennedy) did not want to issue a religion-based license to discriminate against gay people or, more broadly, to avoid complying with all kinds of generally applicable laws. The outcome was a craven compromise, shakily supported by Kennedy's reliance on the odd quirks in the record of the case. The decision was thus exceedingly narrow and based on the peculiar facts of the case, but it effectively invited more cases claiming religious exemption from other laws of general applicability. Though *Cakeshop* was brought as a free speech case from the beginning, and the issue was fully briefed and argued, the majority declined to rule on the issue, kicking the can down the road for the inevitable next case. Only Justice Thomas addressed the free speech issue. His concurring opinion not surprisingly favored the baker's religious views and carved out a religious exemption to civil rights laws. He had no difficulty in finding Phillips to be an artist whose cakes were "speech" protected by the Free Speech Clause.[11] Presumably, originalist Thomas thought the framers would have agreed.

Three weeks after *Cakeshop*, the court vacated a lower court's judgment in *Arlene's Flowers v. State of Washington*, remanding the case for further consideration in light of *Cakeshop*.[12] The case involved a florist who refused for religious reasons to provide flowers for a same-sex marriage. She was found to have violated the state's antidiscrimination law. Like baker Phillips, she raised both free speech and free exercise claims. She and Phillips were represented by the same conservative Christian organization, Alliance Defending Freedom. Bakers and florists will no doubt be followed by jewelers, caterers, tailors and dressmakers, and all kinds of businesses.

* * *

The views of the Roberts Court justices on abortion and the continuing vitality of *Roe v. Wade* have become generally well known over the years. But how they approached *speech* about abortions presented different issues, as shown in an abortion buffer-zone case, *McCullen v. Coakley*.[13]

A Massachusetts law created a thirty-five-foot buffer zone on sidewalks at the entrance to abortion clinics. The state had experienced antiabortion protests that included blocking access to clinics and hassling women entering them to obtain abortions. The buffer zone was designed to deal with this disorder. The

Antiabortion protesters in Portland, Maine.

zone prohibited anyone except patients and clinic employees to be in the zone on the sidewalk. Several antiabortion activists sued, claiming the law violated their First Amendment rights. The court ruled unanimously that the law was unconstitutional, though Justice Scalia said it was a "specious unanimity."

Chief Justice Roberts chose to write the opinion. He denied that the activists who sued were "protesters." He accepted their self-characterization as gentle "sidewalk counselors" who attempted to dissuade women from having abortions by displaying a "caring demeanor, a calm tone of voice, and direct eye contact."[14] Roberts was at pains to point out that their activities took place on public sidewalks—traditional public forums—one of the few places where a speaker can know he or she is "not simply speaking to the choir" and it is possible to persuade or convert some people.

The first question for the court was whether to apply "strict scrutiny" to the state's justifications for the law. That depended on whether the law was content based. The activists argued that the "inevitable effect" of the law was to restrict speech about abortion specifically, as opposed to other subjects.[15] But Roberts concluded the law was not content based; it did not turn on what was said but rather where (in the thirty-five-foot zone). He said the question was not whether the law had a disproportionate effect on antiabortion speech but whether it could be justified without reference to the content of the regulated speech; here, the state had valid interests in maintaining public safety and unobstructed sidewalks.

The activists, however, pointed to the exemption for clinic employees and said this favored one side of the abortion debate. It was therefore viewpoint discrimination, even worse than discrimination based on content. Roberts replied this was not just a carve-out for "escorts" who would reassuringly guide women into the clinics but also included janitors and security guards who would not likely be speaking about anything. Roberts concluded the law was not content based and therefore strict scrutiny was not required.

Roberts then applied the kind of scrutiny the court uses to judge the validity of a law regulating the time, place, or manner of speech, rather than a restriction on its message. He found the Massachusetts law unduly "burdened" the activists' kind of counseling—personal communication and leafletting. And the state had other means of serving its interests: outlawing harassment and intimidation and enforcing laws against obstructing entry and sidewalks. The state failed to justify the "extreme step of closing a traditional public forum to all speakers."

Roberts's opinion infuriated his harder-core conservative brethren. While they technically "concurred" in the outcome—the law was unconstitutional—they thought it was wholly unnecessary even to consider whether the law was content based. They reasoned that it did not matter if it was or not, as all the justices agreed it was unconstitutional because it was not narrowly tailored. Justice Scalia, in particular, thought Roberts was, by finding the law not content based, surreptitiously attempting to make it more likely that some restrictions on antiabortion protests would be upheld. With characteristic hyperbole, Scalia complained the court was "giving abortion-rights advocates a pass when it comes to suppressing the free speech rights of their opponents. There is an entirely separate, abridged edition of the First Amendment applicable to speech about abortion."

Scalia also argued Roberts was wrong on the content-based issue. Because the law applied only to abortion clinics and exempted employees, its obvious purpose, according to Scalia, was to protect clients from having to hear abortion-opposing speech on public sidewalks, a manifestly improper purpose.

Justice Alito wrote separately to make his point that the law discriminated based on viewpoint. He offered plausible hypothetical examples of antiabortion speech by a counselor in the zone (illegal) and prochoice speech by an escort (legal). He concluded: "Speech in favor of the clinic and its work by employees and agents is permitted; speech criticizing the clinic and its work is a crime. This is blatant viewpoint discrimination."

Look at the peculiar lineup of justices in the *McCullen* case. All three women, all prochoice, joined in Chief Justice Roberts's opinion. Why would they do that? A cynic (like Justice Scalia) might say they joined because Roberts agreed not to exercise strict scrutiny. (Strict scrutiny would empower abortion opponents because laws restricting them would more likely be held invalid.) The women on the court must have wanted to leave open the possibility that some restrictions on abortion protests would be upheld. Everyone on the court had to know that the vote could easily have gone 5–4 for Justice Scalia's position. No one knew this better than Scalia, whose bitter opinion was aimed directly at his usual conservative ally, Roberts. Scalia preferred "not to take part in the assembling of an apparent but specious unanimity." His argument that it was unnecessary for the court to decide the content-neutrality-strict-scrutiny issue seems right.

The Roberts compromise made no one happy. It enflamed the other conservative justices who wanted to extend maximum First Amendment protection to abortion protesters. It invalidated a law embraced by liberals to support a woman's right to an abortion. The conservative justices will survive the slight watering down of scrutiny of content-based laws (especially now that they can rely on *Reed*, discussed in chapter 3). And the religious right—Catholic and Evangelical—can correctly claim the court unanimously struck down a law restricting their abortion protests.

*   *   *

In *National Institute of Family and Life Advocates v. Becerra* (*NIFLA*),[16] the court revisited the topic of speech about abortion. The court dealt with a state law requiring antiabortion clinics—self-styled "pregnancy crisis centers"—to post notices informing women where they might find state-provided abortion services.

Concerned that pregnant women might be misled about the services rendered by the clinics and might not be informed about their options, California passed a law regulating "pro-life" clinics that offer services such as pregnancy testing, sonograms, and counseling against abortion. The law required those clinics with a licensed doctor on staff to post a notice, with a telephone number, informing women that the state provides free or low-cost services, including abortions. The law also required clinics without a doctor to post a notice that they were not licensed to provide medical services. The clinics sued, contending the notices abridged their freedom of speech. The state "compelled" the centers to "say" (by posting the notices) what they did not want to say: where and how to obtain an abortion. The state said this was a simple disclosure law that provided useful facts to consumers.

Justice Thomas wrote the 5–4 majority opinion, with the justices splitting along the usual conservative-liberal lines. Thomas began by citing his own opinion in *Reed v. Town of Gilbert* and its expansive notion of what constitutes a content-based regulation of speech. He said the notices here amounted to presumptively unconstitutional content-based regulations. The clinics were required to "provide a government-drafted script" about the availability of state-sponsored services. "One of those services is abortion—the very practice that [the clinics] are devoted to opposing." By requiring information about "state-subsidized abortions—at the same time [the clinics] try to dissuade women from choosing that option,"[17] the notices "plainly 'alter the content' of [the clinics'] speech." Thomas added, relying on *Sorrell*, the drug data case (chapter 3), California's law was "speaker-based" and therefore constitutionally suspect.

Justice Thomas found the state's asserted interests (making sure women were informed of their rights and options and were not misled about what services the pregnancy crisis clinics provided) were unpersuasive, and in any event, the disclosure requirements were not narrowly tailored. He said the notices were not like commercial disclosures the court had approved in the past, in cases in which the disclosures were "purely factual and uncontroversial." According to Thomas, *state*-sponsored abortion was "hardly an uncontroversial topic."

Moreover, the notice to be posted by clinics without doctors was "unjustified" and "unduly burdensome." Required disclosures must remedy a harm that is "potentially real and not purely hypothetical." Thomas found California's interest hypothetical: the state imposed a "government-scripted, speaker-based disclosure requirement that is wholly disconnected from the state's informational interest."

Justice Anthony Kennedy, joined by the other conservative justices, wrote a concurring opinion. He thought the law was "apparent viewpoint discrimination. . . . This law is a paradigmatic example of the serious threat presented when government seeks to impose its own message in the place of individual speech, thought, and expression. For here the state requires primarily pro-life pregnancy centers to promote the state's own preferred message advertising abortions. This compels individuals to contradict their most deeply held beliefs . . . " (This was Kennedy's last opinion, as the next day he announced his resignation from the court.)

Justice Stephen Breyer wrote for the four dissenting justices. Consistent with his general approach to speech cases, he found the "heightened scrutiny" exercised by the court too mechanistic. He said the majority's approach "threatens considerable litigation over the constitutional validity of much, perhaps most, government regulation. Virtually every disclosure law could be considered 'content-based.'" The majority "invites courts around the nation to apply an unpredictable First Amendment to ordinary social and economic regulation. . . . Using the First Amendment to strike down economic and social laws that legislatures long would have thought themselves free to enact will, for the American public, obscure, not clarify, the true value of protecting the freedom of speech." Breyer put his finger on what the Roberts Court majority has done with the Free Speech Clause: make it a weapon that businesses and social conservatives wield to challenge restrictive regulation.

Breyer also criticized the majority's lack of evenhandedness in dealing with the continuing debate over abortion, saying it was "particularly important to interpret the First Amendment so that it applies evenhandedly as between those who disagree so strongly." He reminded the court that it had previously upheld—in an opinion coauthored by Anthony Kennedy—a statutory requirement that abortion doctors tell women about the health risks of abortion, the status of fetal development, and where adoption services could be found.[18] If doctors can be compelled to advise women seeking abortions about adoption services, Breyer reasoned, why can clinics not be compelled to advise pregnant women about abortion services? After all, Breyer concluded, "the rule of law embodies evenhandedness, and 'what is sauce for the goose is normally sauce for the gander.'"

Once again, the court used First Amendment principles in a religious-right case in a way that had the collateral (or quite likely intended) benefit of shielding business from regulation and casting doubt on ordinary commercial disclosure laws. Justice Breyer's fears that the court's new "compelled speech" doctrine would be used to upset ordinary commercial disclosure laws were entirely realistic. Two days after the *NIFLA* case, the court summarily overturned a court of appeals decision that upheld a Berkeley ordinance requiring consumer warnings about possible radiation from cell phones.[19] The court directed the lower court to reconsider this regulation in light of its *NIFLA* decision.

A few months later, the Ninth Circuit Court of Appeals, expressly relying on *NIFLA,* overturned a San Francisco ordinance requiring billboards advertising sugary sodas to contain a warning about the health risks posed by the sodas (e.g., obesity and diabetes).[20] The court ruled that the warnings were "unjustified" and "unduly burdensome," as in *NIFLA*. The US Chamber of Commerce filed an *amicus curiae* brief in the case, showing how quickly the business community picked up on the import of *NIFLA*. The court's compelled-speech locomotive is continuing to gain speed and threatens uncertain numbers of commercial disclosure laws.

The *NIFLA* decision thus does double duty, providing greater protection for both religious and corporate interests. Although its direct beneficiary was the Christian right, the majority's analysis is a powerful antiregulatory weapon in the business arsenal. *NIFLA* and *Janus* (chapter 2), decided a day apart, are close relatives in the pursuit of a *Lochner*esque agenda. Both cases used "compelled speech" as the talisman for employing the Free Speech Clause, rather than *Lochner*'s Due Process Clause, to invalidate democratically enacted laws. Both used reasoning—for example, "unduly burdensome"—that is, capacious enough to allow judges to throw out measures they find unnecessarily meddlesome. Both are prime examples of how the majority justices have weaponized the First Amendment to serve a politically conservative agenda.

FREE SPEECH FOR SOME

Disfavored Speakers and Rulings against Free Speech

The Roberts Court's aggressive deployment of the First Amendment has produced free speech for some—but not for all. The weaponization of the First Amendment as described so far has armed politically conservative corporate interests, antiunion and antiabortion forces, and the Christian right. But the Roberts Court majority has crafted no special weapons for individual traditional free speech claimants. Quite the contrary.

Joseph Frederick was a high school student. Ronald Banks was a state prisoner. Howard Levy was an army doctor. Richard Ceballos was a deputy district attorney. If one put them in a room together, one wonders how long it would take them to discover what they have in common.

Each of them lost his free speech claim in the Supreme Court. Each of them had won in the lower courts. Each of them lost because they belong to a category of citizens who, the Roberts Court says, do not have full First Amendment rights. Each of them lost despite the court's emphatic insistence in *Citizens United* that the First Amendment protects "speech" regardless of the identity of the speaker.

We have seen how the Roberts Court majority gave an expansive reading of "free speech" in order to serve business and politically conservative interests. But when free speech claims were raised by traditional civil liberties claimants, such as public school students, the majority gave the First Amendment a stingy reading.

Morse v. Frederick

In 2002, when the Olympic Torch Relay passed through Juneau, Alaska, directly in front of Juneau-Douglas High School, the school principal released the students to watch the parade. Joseph Frederick, a senior, and some friends were among the crowd of students across the street from the school. They unfurled a fourteen-foot banner that stated, "BONG HITS 4 JESUS."

Deborah Morse, the principal, immediately marched across the street and demanded that the students take the banner down. All but Frederick complied. Morse confiscated the banner and ordered Frederick to report to her office. She suspended him for ten days. She later explained that she thought the banner encouraged illegal drug use in violation of school policy.

Frederick appealed the discipline, but the superintendent of schools ruled that the incident occurred during school hours at a school-sanctioned activity and that Frederick "was not disciplined because the principal of the school 'disagreed' with his message, but because his speech appeared to advocate the use of illegal drugs." Frederick filed suit. The Ninth Circuit Court of Appeals held that the suspension violated his free speech rights.

Before *Morse v. Frederick*,[1] the Supreme Court had decided three "student speech" cases. The precedents were in disarray. The first, *Tinker v. Des Moines Ind. Comm. School Dist.*,[2] in 1969, held that "students do not shed their constitutional rights to freedom of speech or expression at the schoolhouse gate." The court ruled that students could not be disciplined for wearing black armbands to protest the Vietnam War. Student speech could not be suppressed unless school officials reasonably concluded it would "materially and substantially disrupt the work and discipline of the school."

In the second case, *Bethel School Dist. v. Fraser*,³ the court upheld the suspension of a student who gave a political speech at an assembly supporting a candidate for student government. The court said the school had the authority to impose punishment for what it called an "offensively lewd and indecent speech" (even though the nuanced, subtle, humorous speech did not contain a single dirty word). There was no evidence whatever of any disruption caused by the speech, putting *Fraser* at odds with *Tinker*.

In the third case,⁴ the court upheld school officials' right to censor a school newspaper and refuse to publish two articles the students had written. Once again, there was no evidence of any disruption and no attempt to distinguish *Tinker*.

The Roberts Court may have agreed to hear the *Frederick* case in order to harmonize its own precedents and clarify the extent of First Amendment protection for student speech. Unfortunately, the court botched the job.

Chief Justice Roberts decided to write the majority opinion himself. He recounted the facts and results of the three prior cases, and then he punted. He made no attempt to reconcile them or provide any new rule for deciding student speech cases. All he was willing to distill from the cases was that the "rights of students in public school are not automatically coextensive with the rights of adults in other settings."⁵

After describing government efforts to deter drug use by schoolchildren and the Juneau district's antidrug policy, Roberts simply concluded that "the special characteristics of the school environment" and "the governmental interest in stopping student drug abuse . . . allow schools to restrict student expression that they reasonably regard as promoting illegal drug use." Roberts deferred to the school principal's reading of Frederick's banner: it either imperatively called for students to take "bong hits" or it celebrated drug use. Frederick contended the banner did not advocate or celebrate drug use. It was simply "gibberish" intended to get him and his friends on television. Roberts replied that "Gibberish is surely a possible interpretation of the words on the banner, but it is not the only one," and the court would accept the principal's interpretation as reasonable. The court's holding, therefore, was extremely narrow, fact based, and uninformative about how to decide future student speech cases: without any evidence of disruption or actual drug use, school officials can suppress speech they think advocates illegal drug use.

Justices Alito and Kennedy concurred in the ruling against Frederick, but on the basis that officials need to protect the "safety" of the students in their charge and drug use threatens their safety. They indicated that if the banner had been political (e.g., "Legalize Marijuana!") or religious ("Jesus Loves You"), it would have constitutional protection.

Justice Thomas, who dug into history and wrote an originalist concurrence, said historically teachers had the same powers as parents while the children were in school, and students did not have any free speech rights at all. He also lamented the majority's unwillingness to overrule *Tinker* rather than continue to erode its disruption rationale: "We neither overrule it nor offer an explanation of when it operates and when it does not. I am afraid our jurisprudence now says that students have a right to speak in schools except when they don't."

Justice Stevens's dissent accurately pointed out that the court's decision authorizes school officials to engage in viewpoint discrimination: taking sides on an issue. If one can say "Just Say No," suppressing the contrary viewpoint would never be permitted if adults were speaking. Moreover, Stevens said, Frederick had disavowed any pro-drug viewpoint with his "nonsense" banner. And Stevens did not think students would be so stupid as to use drugs simply because of Frederick's banner.

The only principle that can be discerned from the court's decision—given the court's failure to provide any guidance for student speech cases and its leaving its precedents in conflict—is that students comprise a category of speakers who do not have full First Amendment rights.

Beard v. Banks

It is not surprising that the most despised minority in America —prisoners—have not been embraced by the courts and given a full package of constitutional rights. Once convicted and put in the custody of prison officials, their rights are severely curtailed. Of course, prisoners cannot mount mess hall tables and demonstrate against their keepers. But some First Amendment rights are compatible with incarceration. The Roberts Court, however, has made it plain that any such "rights" are almost wholly subject to the discretion of prison officials.

For example, Ronald Banks was held in a segregation unit of a Pennsylvania prison, a unit that housed prisoners whom the authorities deemed the most dangerous or disruptive. The group of about forty prisoners in the unit were prohibited by prison policy from receiving or possessing newspapers, magazines, or personal family photographs. None. They joined in a class action and claimed this policy violated the First Amendment.[6]

The Roberts Court upheld the policy, saying the Constitution permits greater restriction of citizens' rights in prison than in the free world. The only question was whether the restriction was "reasonably related to legitimate penological interests." There was no need for the state to show a compelling interest or narrow tailoring, or any actual harm whatever. The officials said the prison policy was needed to "motivate better behavior," and the court deferred to their judgment. (Deferring to officials' judgment is, of course, the opposite of exercising serious scrutiny.)

Justice Stevens dissented. He noted the improve-behavior-by-deprivation rationale had "no limiting principle." It would furnish a rational basis for deprivation of any right, and the more important the right, the stronger the justification for the deprivation.

The *Banks* decision makes plain the court's view that prisoners, as a class, do not have full First Amendment rights. The court reiterated this in *Citizens United*, when it cited an earlier case also holding that prisoners are a category of citizens whose speech could be limited or suppressed. (The earlier case was *Jones v. North Carolina Prisoners Labor Union*.[7] The court in that decision upheld regulations prohibiting prisoners from soliciting other prisoners to join a union.)

Garcetti v. Ceballos

Richard Ceballos was a Los Angeles deputy district attorney with some supervisorial responsibilities. A defense lawyer in a criminal case asked Ceballos to review an affidavit submitted to support a search warrant. Ceballos did so, and found it contained false statements. Ceballos wrote a memo to his superiors, recommending the prosecution be dropped. His bosses disagreed. They refused to dismiss the case, and then they reassigned Ceballos to a lower position, transferred him to a different office, and denied him a promotion.

Ceballos sued, contending the retaliatory action punished him for exercising his right to free speech. The memo was the "speech."[8]

Justice Kennedy wrote the opinion for the 5–4 conservative majority. He acknowledged that public employees do not surrender all their First Amendment rights. The amendment protects an employee's right to speak "as a citizen" on matters of public concern. But it does not protect against discipline for speech within the scope of his or her duties. Kennedy said government employers "need a significant degree of control over their employees' words." Without that control, government could not efficiently provide public services.

Kennedy said the controlling fact in Ceballos's case was that "his expressions were made pursuant to his duties as a calendar deputy," not about issues of public importance. Kennedy concluded: "We hold that when public employees make statements pursuant to their official duties, the employees are not speaking as citizens for First Amendment purposes, and the Constitution does not insulate their communications from employer discipline."

In other words, public employee speech is protected only if it is engaged in as a private citizen and not if it is expressed as part of the employee's duties.

Putting aside whether the court's rule is workable in the sense that courts will be able to distinguish an employee's views as citizen from his or her views as employee, the court made clear that public employees, as a class, do not have full First Amendment protection. This too was reiterated in *Citizens United* when the court cited an earlier case as indicating that public employees, like students and prisoners, have limited free speech protection. (The earlier case was *Civil Service Com-*

mission v. Letter Carriers,[9] which upheld the Hatch Act prohibition on federal civil service employees taking "an active part in political management or in political campaigns." "Partisan political conduct" was banned.)

Parker v. Levy

Howard Levy was an army doctor stationed at an army hospital in South Carolina during the Vietnam War. He was opposed to the war on ethical grounds. He refused to train Special Forces aides for service there, and he made public statements to African American enlisted men, including the following:

> The United States is wrong in being involved in the Vietnam War. I would refuse to go to Vietnam if ordered to do so. I don't see why any colored soldier would go to Vietnam: they should refuse to go to Vietnam, and, if sent, should refuse to fight because they are discriminated against and denied their freedom in the United States, and they are sacrificed and discriminated against in Vietnam by being given all the hazardous duty and they are suffering the majority of casualties. If I were a colored soldier, I would refuse to go to Vietnam, and if I were a colored soldier and were sent, I would refuse to fight. Special Forces personnel are liars and thieves and killers of peasants and murderers of women and children.

Levy was court marshaled for, among other things, "conduct unbecoming an officer and a gentleman." He was convicted.

In 1974, the Supreme Court upheld the conviction, based on Levy's status as a member of the military.[10] Justice Rehnquist said:

> While the members of the military are not excluded from the protection granted by the First Amendment, the different character of the military community and of the military mission requires a different application of those

protections. The fundamental necessity for obedience, and the consequent necessity for imposition of discipline, may render permissible within the military that which would be constitutionally impermissible outside it.

The *Levy* case obviously predated the Roberts Court. The case is included here because it was cited by name by the Roberts Court in *Citizens United* as limiting the First Amendment rights of military personnel.

*　*　*

Thus, the Roberts Court has held that the government can restrict or punish the speech—even political speech—of at least four very large categories of citizens. This is inconsistent with the main theme of *Citizens United,* that the First Amendment protects "speech" regardless of the identity of the speaker. In *Citizens United,* Justice Kennedy denied there was any inconsistency. He did not attempt to distinguish the cases discussed above on their facts. Instead, he simply asserted, "The Court has upheld a narrow [sic] class of speech restrictions that operate to the disadvantage of certain persons, but these rulings were based on an interest in allowing governmental entities to perform their functions." He said the cases "stand only for the proposition that there are certain governmental functions that cannot operate without some restrictions on particular kinds of speech."

This simplistic, conclusionary ipse dixit is not a satisfactory explanation of why corporations should be able to spend money on elections but students, prisoners, public employees, and military personnel—millions of American citizens—can be restricted from engaging in pure political speech.

It may be worth noting that, although this was not recognized by the court, all four of the cases of disfavored speakers could be said to involve an institutional interest in maintaining *discipline*. That is, schools need to enforce order in the classroom and the educational environment; prisons need to keep prisoners from escaping, rebelling, or endangering others; the military needs soldiers to obey orders; and government needs to make sure its own employees do not contradict policy. Enthroning government as disciplinarian does not seem an adequate basis for limiting the political speech of real human beings while allowing corporations to speak with their money.

Rulings against Free Speech

Chief Justice Roberts's first opinion in a First Amendment case, and his first rejection of a free speech claim, came in *Rumsfeld v. Forum for Academic and Institutional Rights*,[11] handed down on March 6, 2006. The case involved law schools that objected to the military's "Don't ask, don't tell" policy on gays in the armed services. The schools challenged a federal law requiring them to allow military recruiters on campus on the same terms as other recruiters or else lose federal funding for their entire institutions. The schools made somewhat strained First Amendment contentions, complaining, for example, that having to send out scheduling emails amounted to impermissible "compelled" speech. Roberts said the law "neither limits what law schools may say nor requires them to say anything."

Moreover, the law regulated "conduct, not speech," and the conduct (hosting recruiters) was not "inherently expressive." Roberts said the academics were attempting to "stretch" First Amendment doctrines too far and "exaggerating the reach of our First Amendment precedents." The Roberts Court reinvigorated the "compelled speech" doctrine and implemented it with a vengeance in the *Janus* and *NIFLA* cases (chapters 2 and 4, respectively) at the behest of antiunion and antiabortion forces.

In 2010, Chief Justice Roberts wrote the only terrorism speech opinion of the twenty-first century. It was a timid effort, and it came out the wrong way.

After 9/11, Congress made it a crime to provide "material support" to designated foreign terrorist organizations. The law defines "material support" to include any "service" or "expert advice or assistance," as well as more obvious and tangible kinds of support like money, lodging, false documentation, weapons, and transportation. The secretary of state designates entities considered to be foreign terrorist organizations. Among the thirty designated organizations is the Kurdistan Workers' Party. Its violent history and designation were not in dispute.

Two American citizens and several US organizations sued then-Attorney General Eric Holder, challenging the material-support law. They wished to provide support for the humanitarian and political activities of the Kurdish organization. Specifically, they wanted to train members on "how to use humanitarian and international law to peacefully resolve disputes," engage in political advocacy on behalf of Kurds living in Turkey, teach members how to petition the United Nations for relief, and use legal expertise in negotiating peace agreements. They claimed the law did not apply to these activities, and, if it did, it violated the First Amendment.

In *Holder v. Humanitarian Law Project*,[12] Chief Justice Roberts ruled that these activities—though pure speech—did constitute "material support" and the law did not violate the First Amendment. He interpreted the statute as applying only to support that is coordinated with or under the direction of a designated terrorist organization. It does not apply to independent advocacy. (Thus, it would be legal for a person to write or advocate in support of al-Qaeda or ISIS as long as this is done independently, somewhat reminiscent of the "independent expenditures" reasoning of *Citizens United*.)

Justice Ruth Bader Ginsburg.

Roberts determined that the government had an "urgent interest of the highest order" in preventing terrorist activity and that the material-support provision was sufficiently tailored to serve the government's interest. Roberts said all kinds of assistance were "fungible" in the sense that whatever services were provided would free up organization resources that could be devoted to nonhumanitarian and perhaps terrorist activities. Moreover, providing expert assistance would lend "legitimacy" to the organizations and allow them to pretend to be negotiating while in fact plotting violence. Roberts recognized these were "empirical" questions but was willing to defer to the government's judgment on them, basically taking the government's word that unhappy consequences would flow from allowing any assistance to terrorist organizations. (This kind of deference is the exact opposite of "strict scrutiny.")[13]

Justice Breyer dissented, joined by Justices Ginsburg and Sotomayor. (Elena Kagan argued the case for the government when she was solicitor general, before being appointed to replace Justice Stevens on the court.) Justice Breyer pointed out that even filing an *amicus curiae* brief would violate the statute as interpreted by the court (assuming the brief was coordinated with the organization, as *amicus* briefs commonly are). He said the law should have been interpreted to require an intent by the service provider to further the organization's unlawful terrorist actions, not its humanitarian or political activities. Breyer said the government had failed to present any evidence that the kind of activities the Humanitarian Law Project wanted to engage in would in fact further the terrorist objectives of the organizations. The project's speech-related efforts were not "fungible" like money, and the court's fears were speculative, not fact based. Moreover, the court's allowing independent advocacy was inconsistent with its claim that the project's support would lend undesirable "legitimacy" to the organizations.

In essence, though not in name, Breyer was engaging in the inclusiveness analysis the court has frequently used in First Amendment cases. That is, he demonstrated that the statute was overinclusive in that it outlawed nonterrorist speech and underinclusive in that independent advocacy was permitted, so the law did not solve the problem. Being over- and underinclusive means the law is not narrowly tailored to serve the government's interest. The *Holder* case is an example of the Roberts Court rigorously employing one mode of First Amendment analysis in one case and ignoring it in another.

The Roberts Court manages to bestow free speech protection on corporations seeking to avoid regulation, corporations wishing to spend without limit on elections, Christian right litigants trying to avoid antidiscrimination laws, and antiabortion activists trying to overturn *Roe v. Wade,* while at the same

COMBATTING GOVERNMENT OVERREACH
The Court's Libertarian Rulings

The Roberts Court decisions discussed above involve *Loch-ner*ian deployment of the First Amendment to serve the anti-regulatory interests of business and the Christian right. Other free speech decisions by the court form a different, but not inconsistent, pattern: libertarian rulings.

The Federalist Society, the intellectual home of the Roberts Court's politically conservative majority, says it is composed of "conservatives and libertarians."[1] One can be conservative without being libertarian. For example, many conservatives oppose abortion and want government to make it illegal. That's the antithesis of libertarian thought in that it calls for enlisting government to overrule a woman's choice not to bear a child. Similarly, opposition to same-sex marriage is antilibertarian, in that it asks government to dictate to whom one can be married. Opposing immigration is another conservative but not libertarian issue. Libertarians seek to minimize government involvement in private life.

Historically, the Supreme Court's First Amendment jurisprudence was a refuge for the unpopular speech of protestors and eccentrics. Many of the court's most memorable rulings were essentially libertarian, freeing individuals to think as they wish and say what they think—to speak truth to power. The great opinions by Justices Holmes and Brandeis were in this vein.[2] Government was not allowed to suppress and punish speech it considered subversive. These libertarian rulings were, in Justice Kagan's words, some of the "better things" the amendment was meant for.

The Roberts Court has not abandoned this libertarian tradition. It has, for example, found First Amendment protection for a bigoted funeral protest, a racial insult, a lie, gruesome pictures, violent video games, and a Tea Party T-shirt. The speech in most of these cases was offensive to the great majority of citizens. It had very little to do with ascertaining the truth about any issue, promoting a self-governing democracy, or protecting individual dignity. Consistent with the Roberts Court majority's use of free speech principles to advance a conservative political agenda, the beneficiaries of these rulings included religious fundamentalists, businesses selling depictions of violence, and the Tea Party. But at the same time, the decisions are largely consonant with traditional First Amendment analysis rather than stretching the analysis for deregulatory purposes. Thus, alongside its signature embrace of First Amendment arguments empowering business and the Christian right, the Roberts Court has not entirely forsaken the "better things."

Funeral Protests: *Snyder v. Phelps*

Reverend Fred W. Phelps founded the Westboro Baptist Church in Topeka, Kansas, and for decades was its only pastor. The congregation had a few dozen members, most of whom were Phelps's children, grandchildren, and in-laws. The church had a "fire and brimstone" fundamentalist religious faith. Among the members' beliefs was that God hates homosexuality and punishes America for its tolerance of homosexuality, particularly in the military. Church members picketed hundreds of military funerals to publicize their religious viewpoint.

In 2006, Marine Lance Corporal Matthew A. Snyder was killed in Iraq in the line of duty. His father chose a Catholic church in Maryland for the funeral and placed notices in local newspapers with the time and location of the funeral.

Phelps, with two of his daughters and four of his grand-children, announced they would travel to Maryland and picket the funeral. Recognizing there might be community reaction, they also notified the police. They complied with police directions to stay a certain distance from the church. While picketing, they carried large homemade signs with messages such as "God Hates the USA," "Fag troops," "Priests rape boys," "You're going to hell," and "Thank God for dead soldiers." This was, by any definition, hate speech, targeting people because of their sexual orientation and religion.

Although he knew of Phelps's presence and picketing, the Marine's father did not actually see the signs until he viewed a television news program later that day. He was grievously upset. He sued Phelps and the Westboro church for intentional infliction of emotional injury and invasion of privacy. The jury awarded $5 million in damages.

Phelps and the church appealed and won a reversal in the court of appeals. Phelps, ably represented by one of his daughters who happened to be a lawyer, landed in the Supreme Court.[3]

Despite the hateful, ignorant, wrong-headed speech at issue, this was an easy First Amendment case. The court ruled 8–1 that the Phelps protestors were protected by the First Amendment. Chief Justice Roberts assigned himself to write the opinion. The opinion was very fact specific and narrow, and changing any one of the facts might have changed the outcome.

Roberts said the decision turned "largely" on whether the protestors' speech related to issues of "public concern." Roberts acknowledged that while the protestors' messages "may fall short of refined social or political commentary, the issues they highlight—the political and moral conduct of the United

States and its citizens, the fate of our Nation, homosexuality in the military, and scandals involving the Catholic clergy—are matters of public import." Crucially, it was the content of the protestors' speech that the Marine's father objected to: he was upset by what the signs said. His lawyer admitted at oral argument that he would have no case if the signs had said "God Bless America" or "God Bless Our Veterans."

Among the other facts emphasized by the chief justice were that the protestors stayed one thousand feet away from the church on a public sidewalk where they had a right to be and to speak, that they were not visible from the funeral, and that they did not disrupt it.

Justice Samuel Alito was the lone dissenter. He seemed to be morally offended by the protestors' conduct (and most Americans would agree). He noted the protestors were free to express their views in books, articles, and videos and to speak in public, on television, radio, and the Internet. But it did not follow, for Alito, that the protestors could "intentionally inflict severe emotional injury on private persons at a time of intense emotional sensitivity by launching vicious verbal attacks that make no contribution to public debate."

Perhaps in response to Alito's dissent and doubtless cognizant of the unpopularity of the protestors' speech and conduct, Chief Justice Roberts concluded his opinion for the court with the following:

> Speech is powerful. It can stir people to action, move them to tears of both joy and sorrow, and—as it did here—inflict great pain. On the facts before us, we cannot react to that pain by punishing the speaker. As a Nation we have chosen a different course—to protect even hurtful speech on public issues to ensure that we do not stifle public debate.

Thus, this hate speech was protected from liability. The decision (with the possible exception of Alito's dissent) clearly was not attributable to the individual justices' religious affiliations. Although religious fundamentalists won, it was not because the court stretched the First Amendment to validate their beliefs. Nor was the speech protected because of its contribution to the search for truth or to facilitate our self-governing democracy. Indeed, its main claim for constitutional protection was its very unpopularity and distrust of government to exercise sound judgment in determining what speech touching on public issues is permissible. The decision was about as libertarian, antimajoritarian, and politically incorrect as any decision of the Roberts Court.

Crush Videos: *United States v. Stevens*

If there is speech less worthy of constitutional protection than bigoted funeral protests, perhaps it is pictures of cruelty to animals. But the Roberts Court's decision on this topic contains some saving graces that are important for preserving more worthy kinds of speech that government might like to suppress.

Apparently concerned about "crush videos" that feature the torture and killing of helpless animals and appeal to persons with a specific sexual fetish, Congress passed a law prohibiting the creation, sale, or possession for commercial purposes of certain "depictions" of animal cruelty. The law applied to any depiction "in which a living animal is intentionally maimed, mutilated, tortured, wounded or killed." The law exempted depictions with "serious religious, political, scientific, educational, journalistic, historical, or artistic value." Violation of the law was punishable by up to five years in prison. When President Bill Clinton signed the law, he instructed the Justice Department to prosecute only cases involving depictions appealing to the "prurient interest," as is required in prosecutions for "obscenity."

Robert J. Stevens sold videos of pit bulls in dogfights and attacking other animals. Some of the videos came from Japan, where dogfighting is apparently legal; some were older American dogfights; and some involved pit bulls hunting wild boar and killing a farm pig. No crush videos; no prurient interest. Stevens was convicted and sentenced to thirty-seven months in prison.

In an opinion by Chief Justice Roberts, the court found the law unconstitutional.[4] Roberts first addressed the government's argument that such depictions have so little social value that they should be treated as a category, like obscenity or libel, completely without First Amendment protection. The government proposed a simple balancing test: whether a category of speech is protected depends on balancing its value against its social costs.

The proposal was resoundingly rejected by Chief Justice Roberts. He said this "free-floating test" for First Amendment coverage was "startling and dangerous." The amendment's guarantee is not limited to categories of speech that "survive an ad hoc balancing of relative social costs and benefits." He added, "The First Amendment itself reflects a judgment by the American people that the benefits of its restrictions on the Government outweigh the costs. Our Constitution forecloses any attempt to revise that judgment simply on the basis that some speech is not worth it." The government cannot be permitted "to imprison any speaker so long as his speech is deemed valueless or unnecessary." The chief justice said there was no "freewheeling authority to declare new categories of speech outside the scope of the First Amendment."

Having demolished the government's categorical contention, Roberts then followed conventional First Amendment analysis. Because the law restricted speech on the basis of content, it was "presumptively invalid," and the government had the burden of demonstrating the restriction would serve a "compelling" government interest and was narrowly tailored to serve the interest. Roberts did not pay much attention to whether the government interest was "compelling." Instead, he concluded the law was overbroad, in that it criminalized a substantial amount of protected speech. For example, the law did not in fact require that the depicted conduct be "cruel"; wounding and killing are not necessarily cruel. So, hunting videos would be illegal. Other examples of depictions of lawful conduct that might run afoul of the ban included pictures of bullfights, rodeos, safaris, and slaughterhouses.

The government also tried to save the statute by arguing that its exceptions clause—exempting from punishment depictions that have "serious religious, political, scientific, educational, journalistic, historical, or artistic value"—ensured that speech with some social value would not be criminalized. Again, the chief justice rejected the government's contention. He pointed out that "*Most* of what we say to one another" lacks the listed values but "is still sheltered from government regulation." Speech with purely entertainment value, discussions about the weather, sports, neighborhood gossip, and all kinds of folk wisdom might be examples. The court thus squelched another dangerous legislative technique, one that would have stood our system of freedoms on its head. Under our system, we are free to say what we please unless some very important competing value requires a restriction; this contrasts with totalitarian regimes under which citizens' expressive freedoms are restricted unless the government grants permission. Roberts said, "the First Amendment protects against the Government; it does not leave us at the mercy of *noblesse oblige*." Thus, Congress is not free to prohibit various kinds of speech simply by providing exceptions for what it considers speech with redeeming social value.

Justice Alito was again the sole dissenter. He said the law was not meant to suppress speech but to prevent horrific acts of animal cruelty in a "form of depraved entertainment." He would have treated depictions of animal cruelty like child pornography: the very production of the images requires commission of a crime.

Once again, the court invoked the First Amendment to protect "speech" that has nothing to do with ascertaining the truth in the marketplace of ideas and that does not enhance our effort to make a self-governing democracy work. Yet *Stevens* made a useful contribution toward protecting other kinds of unpopular speech that governments—federal, state, and local—might like to suppress. The ruling that government and judges cannot declare new *kinds* of speech valueless, and the ruling that government cannot justify a ban on disfavored speech by including a clause saving specified kinds of government-approved speech, are sound First Amendment principles. To be sure, the principles can be used to benefit business interests, as they were in the video games case, considered next. But there is no reason to believe these principles were articulated specially to serve the conservative political agenda.

Violent Video Games: *Brown v. Entertainment Merchants*

Did James Madison and the framers expect the First Amendment to protect popular entertainment? Just as in *Citizens United,* in which Justices Scalia and Stevens could not locate dispositive historical evidence of whether the framers meant the First Amendment to protect corporations, so it is with the framers' intent about popular entertainment. Their concern was core political speech, the kind essential to a self-governing democracy. But if they paused to think about it, probably they would have wanted the amendment to safeguard literature, poetry, and other art forms against government censorship, at least censorship by the federal government. Still, they could not have foreseen applying the amendment to popular culture and communications on the fantastic new technologies developed in the twentieth and twenty-first centuries.

As each new medium of communication has come on the scene—from dime novels to movies, comic books, television, rap music lyrics, the Internet, and video games—legislatures have attempted to shield America's children from its corrupting influence. Every attempt has failed. It is now well established that the First Amendment protects literature, art, cartoons, movies, plays, and, to some extent, commercial advertising and topless dancing.

California's attempt to protect kids from what it saw as the harmful influences of violent video games (studies show a high percentage of high school boys play video games for many hours a week, and some of the violent games are among the most popular) wound up before the Roberts Court, and the case scrambled the court's usual ideological lineup.

In 2005, the California legislature enacted a law making it illegal to sell or rent a violent video game to a minor. The law defined "violent video game" to mean a game in which the range of options available to a player includes "killing, maiming, dismembering, or sexually assaulting an image of a human being," if those acts are depicted in a way that meets the following three tests:

> (i) A reasonable person, considering the game as a whole, would find appeals to a deviant or morbid interest of minors;

> (ii) It is patently offensive to prevailing standards in the community as to what is suitable for minors; and

> (iii) It causes the game, as a whole, to lack serious literary, artistic, political, or scientific value for minors.

(This definition of the games that could not be sold to minors was a parody of the Supreme Court's longstanding definition of "obscenity."[5] To be legally obscene, the material must appeal to the "prurient interest," it must be "patently offensive" in its depiction of sexual acts, and it must lack "serious literary, artistic, political, or scientific value." As if that definition were not vague, confusing, and incoherent enough, the California legislature substituted an appeal to "a deviant or morbid interest" for "prurient" interest, and it tacked on to each of the three obscenity prongs something about "minors." That clumsiness alone was enough to get Justices Alito and Roberts to condemn the law as impermissibly vague.)

The legislature stated that it had two main purposes: "preventing violent, aggressive, and antisocial behavior;" and "preventing psychological harm to minors who play violent video games." When the video game industry challenged the law in court, the state could not come up with evidence that playing video games caused violence—a causal link between playing and violent behavior—and therefore abandoned the first purpose. It focused on "the actual harm to the brain of the child playing the video game."

The video game industry prevailed in the lower courts. During oral argument before the Roberts Court, the state faced a barrage of hostile questions and comments. Justice Ruth Bader Ginsburg asked the state's lawyer, "If you are supposing a category of violent materials dangerous to children, then how do you cut it off at video games? What about films? What about comic books? Grimm's fairy tales?" Justice Scalia, flaunting his originalist thinking, remarked to the state's lawyer, "It was always understood that the freedom of speech did not include obscenity. It has never been understood that the freedom of speech did not include portrayals of violence. You are asking us to create a whole new prohibition which the American people never ratified when they ratified the First Amendment. . . . What's after violence? Drinking? Smoking? Movies that show smoking can't be shown to children? . . . Are we to sit day by day to decide what else will be made an exception from the First Amendment?" (This prompted Justice Alito to remark that "I think what Justice Scalia wants to know is what James Madison thought about video games.") Justice Anthony Kennedy asked the industry's lawyer, "Why shouldn't violence be treated the same as obscenity?"

In *Brown v. Entertainment Merchants Ass'n*,[6] the court ruled 7–2 that the state law violated the First Amendment. Justice Scalia wrote the majority opinion. In an unusual ideological split, Scalia was joined by three "liberal" justices (Ginsburg, Sotomayor, and Kagan) plus Anthony Kennedy; two conservatives, Justice Alito and Chief Justice Roberts, agreed the law was invalid (because it was too vague, an issue not reached by the majority) but otherwise disagreed with Scalia's opinion; Justice Thomas dissented from his conservative soulmate's opinion; Justice Breyer also dissented.

The opinion was vintage Scalia: acerbic, confrontational, imperious, dismissive of anyone's contrary point of view, and a formidable weapon in the First Amendment arsenal. It moved the court in the direction he wanted it to go.

The first question was whether video games qualify as "speech" for First Amendment purposes. Justice Scalia said that though the Free Speech Clause "exists principally to protect discourse on public matters," it "is difficult to distinguish politics from entertainment, and dangerous to try." Like protected books, plays, and movies, "video games communicate ideas—and even social messages—through many familiar literary devices (such as characters, dialogue, plot, and music) and through features distinctive to the medium (such as the player's interaction with the virtual world). That suffices to confer First Amendment protection."

The state argued that violent video games constitute an exception to the freedom of speech, a category—like obscenity—that deserves no First Amendment protection. Justice Scalia concluded, however, that this argument was foreclosed by the *Stevens* animal cruelty precedent. Justice Scalia said that under *Stevens*, "new categories of unprotected speech may not be added to the list by a legislature that concludes certain speech is too harmful to be tolerated." Absent a history of nonprotection (as for obscenity, perjury, or libel), no new category can be created simply by weighing the value of particular speech against its social costs.

Scalia emphatically denied there was any history of restricting children's access to depictions of violence. To the contrary, he noted that the books we give children to read, or read to them, "contain no shortage of gore." He recounted the violent content of *Grimm's Fairy Tales*, *Cinderella*, *Hansel and Gretel*, and books on high school reading lists such as Homer's *Odysseus*, Dante's *Inferno*, and *Lord of the Flies*.

So there was no historical warrant for shielding children from violent material. Nor could depictions of violence be treated as "obscene." The court has defined obscenity to include only erotic material and "violence is not part of the obscenity that the Constitution permits to be regulated."

Moreover, and again following *Stevens*, Scalia said tacking on a savings clause purporting to rescue speech with government-approved value (artistic, literary, etc.) does not save a statute from condemnation.

Since violent video games were not categorically unprotected, and since the California law restricted speech on the basis of its content, standard First Amendment analysis applied. A content restriction is presumptively unconstitutional and that puts the burden on the state to satisfy "strict scrutiny." The government has to demonstrate that a content-based restriction is justified by a "compelling government interest" and is narrowly tailored to serve that interest. Justice Scalia applied this scrutiny with a vengeance.

Scalia was unpersuaded that video games were a serious problem. He pointed to the state's concession that it could not show "a direct causal link between violent video games and harm to minors." While some psychological studies may show "some effect on children's feelings of aggression," these effects "are both small and indistinguishable from effects produced by other media," including Bugs Bunny cartoons on television. (Scalia dropped a footnote ridiculing the state's evidence, which read: "One study, for example, found that children who had just finished playing violent video games were more likely to fill in the blank letter in 'explo_e' with a 'd' (so that it reads 'explode') than with an 'r' ('explore'). The prevention of this phenomenon, which might have been anticipated with common sense, is not a compelling state interest.")

Justice Scalia also reasoned that the law was "underinclusive" in singling out the purveyors of video games for disfavored treatment while booksellers, cartoonists, and movie and television producers trafficking in violence were not restricted. Moreover, while the state has the power to protect children from actual harm, it has "no free-floating power to restrict the ideas to which children may be exposed." Justice Scalia also found the law "overinclusive," in that it prohibited minors whose parents did not care, or actually wanted their children to have the games, from buying the games.

Justice Alito strongly disagreed. He and Chief Justice Roberts concurred in the result, but only on the ground the statute was unconstitutionally "vague": it gave no fair notice of what was prohibited. Alito pointed to the references to terms like "deviant" and "morbid interest." The vagueness was compounded by lumping together toddlers and relatively sophisticated adolescents as "minors."

Alito did his own research into some of the most notorious games and found the violence "astounding." He noted that "victims are dismembered, decapitated, disemboweled, set on fire, and chopped into little pieces. . . . Blood gushes, splatters, and pools." Alito revealed his personal revulsion at the immoral lessons taught by some of the games: "There is no antisocial theme too base for some in the video game industry to exploit," pointing to games allowing the player to reenact the murders at Columbine and Virginia Tech, the assassination of President Kennedy, and to engage in ethnic cleansing by choosing to "gun down African-Americans, Latinos, or Jews."

Scalia acknowledged that "Reading Dante is unquestionably more cultured and intellectually edifying than playing Mortal Kombat." But he said these differences are not constitutional ones: "Justice Alito recounts all these disgusting video games in order to disgust us—but disgust is not a valid basis for restricting expression." Scalia added, "Crudely violent games, tawdry TV shows and cheap novels and magazines are no less forms of speech than The Divine Comedy, and restrictions on them must survive strict scrutiny." He went on to surmise "the real reason for governmental proscription"—and probably Alito's objections—was the *"ideas"* expressed by the games rather than their supposed harm to minors. It is likely both the California legislators and Alito were animated more by their moral objections to the themes than by the prospect of actual harm caused to young gamers.

Justice Thomas also parted company with his originalist ally and mentor. Thomas wrote a long, impassioned dissenting opinion, concluding that history showed the framers would not have protected speech directed at children that their parents would not want them exposed to. Scalia brushed this off in a footnote. Without abandoning his own originalist viewpoint, Scalia said Thomas's thesis that children do not have "any constitutional right to speak or be spoken to without their parents' consent" was without "historical warrant" and, in any event, the California law did not enforce parental authority over children's speech; it supplanted it with government authority.

Justice Breyer also dissented. His opinion was consistent with his reluctance to exercise strict scrutiny in free speech cases. Here, he was concerned about some psychological studies indicating that playing violent games seems to affect kids' feelings of aggression. Breyer was reluctant to say the state legislature could not rely on them. He acknowledged that no one has shown a causal effect between playing the games and actual aggression, and that many studies contradict the ones he dug up. But Breyer was willing to give government the benefit of the doubt (not a salutary approach in a First Amendment case).

Breyer made an interesting point about what he saw as an "anomaly" in First Amendment law. Under the court's precedents, a state can prohibit the sale to minors of magazines containing nudity.[7] Breyer thought it made no sense to forbid selling a thirteen-year-old boy a magazine with an image of a nude woman while protecting the sale of a game in which he can bind, gag, torture, and kill her. "What kind of First Amendment would permit the government to protect children by restricting sales of such an extremely violent video game *only* when the woman—bound, gagged, tortured, and killed—is also *topless?*"

Indeed, what does it say about our culture that we are legally so squeamish about sexual material but quite willing to allow our children to wallow in violent material? Justice Scalia was characteristically sarcastic about the legislature's concerns, unwilling to accept the legislature's judgment that video games cause harm, and dismissive in his treatment of the social science evidence. This all contrasts with his own approach just two years earlier in a broadcast "indecency" case[8] in which he enthusiastically accepted—without *any* empirical evidence—the government's contention that exposing children to "indecent" words in television and radio broadcasts created cognizable harm to children. One wonders why Justice Scalia—and the court—would be more tolerant of violent materials than sexual materials.

What accounts for the unusual ideological split in the case? Here we have the politically conservative Scalia writing an opinion joined by three liberals plus Justice Kennedy. Here we find Alito strongly disagreeing with Scalia, his usual conservative ally. Here we have Justice Thomas, the other avowed originalist, parting company with Scalia. And here we have Justice Breyer abandoning the other liberals on the court. The scrambled lineup probably has to do with the fact that this was not a case with partisan political implications. It concerned one's tolerance for expression that disturbs many people and one's trust in government to make sound judgments about what is good for us. Unwillingness to accept offensive, unsettling speech, and faith in government's ability to sort out worthy from unworthy speech are the end of free speech.

Of course, the case can be viewed as just another Roberts Court effort to use the First Amendment to further the interests of big business—in this case, the immensely profitable video games industry. That it was. But it was more. The majority opinion was an impressive demonstration of how potent an engine, for better or for worse, the modern First Amendment has become.

A Constitutional Right to Lie? *United States v. Alvarez*

When Xavier Alvarez's case reached the Supreme Court,[9] his lawyers filed a very unusual brief. It began:

> Xavier Alvarez lied. He lied when he claimed to have played professional hockey for the Detroit Red Wings. He lied when he claimed to be married to a Mexican starlet whose appearance in public caused paparazzi to swoon. He lied when he claimed to be an engineer. He lied when he claimed to have rescued the American ambassador during the Iranian hostage crisis, and when he said that he was shot going back to grab the American flag. . . . But none of those lies were crimes.

The brief went on to say that when Alvarez was elected to a Southern California water district board, he introduced himself at the first meeting and said: "I'm a retired Marine of 25 years. I retired in the year 2001. Back in 1987, I was awarded the Congressional Medal of Honor. I got wounded many times by the same guy. I'm still around."

Other than being "still around," these were all lies. Alvarez had never served in the military, been wounded, or received a medal of any kind. His lies were almost immediately exposed, and he was investigated by the FBI. He was charged with violating the Stolen Valor Act of 2005, which provided that "Whoever falsely represents himself or herself, verbally or in writing, to have been awarded any decoration or medal authorized by Congress" is subject to imprisonment for six months. If the medal was the Congressional Medal of Honor, the prison term doubled to a year.

Alvarez entered a plea of guilty, reserving his right to appeal. He was sentenced to a year in prison. His only defense was the First Amendment. The court of appeals held that this clear, specific, and targeted law was unconstitutional.

In the Roberts Court on the government's appeal, the government made the same kind of argument as in the *Stevens* and the video games cases: false statements of fact have no social value and constitute a category of speech with no First Amendment protection at all.

The court ruled in Alvarez's favor, finding the Stolen Valor Act violated the Free Speech Clause. Justice Anthony Kennedy wrote the opinion. He had to acknowledge that the court had frequently said falsehoods had no free speech value. But that was in cases involving perjury, defamation, or fraud, in which there was an element of falsity. The court had never said false statements, per se, lack First Amendment protection, yet the Stolen Valor Act "targets falsity and nothing more." Once again, the court refused to add to the historically recognized categories of unprotected speech. And once again the court extended protection to speech having no claim to enhancing the search for truth or promoting democratic self-rule.

So why protect Alvarez's lie? Kennedy pointed out the act's almost unlimited reach. It applied to dishonestly bragging about a medal at any time, in any place, to any person (whether uttered from a barstool, whispered at home, or shouted from a rooftop). And it applied regardless of whether anyone was harmed, regardless of whether the braggart sought or obtained any benefit and even if no one believed the boast. In short, there was no limiting principle. Allowing a law like this to be enforced would invite government to compile lists of the subjects—such as academic credentials, military service, business experience—citizens could be forbidden from lying about.

Kennedy accepted uncritically that the government had a "compelling" interest in preserving respect for the medal and its recipients and the integrity of the military honors system. (The court virtually never second-guesses the validity of the interest proffered by the government.) But he put some real teeth into the "narrow tailoring" part of the court's scrutiny. Kennedy said the government must show that the speech restriction is "actually necessary" to serve its interest. There must be a "direct causal link" between the restriction and the harm to be prevented. But the government had produced no evidence showing that respect for medals or medal winners was diluted by false claims.

Given that Alvarez could have legally burned, defaced, mutilated, or disparaged a medal, or called actual recipients cowards, or damned the government and its wars, or said he should have received the medal, there was no reason to believe the act fixed any problem.

Nor did the government show that counterspeech would be ineffective to serve its interests. It was, after all, immediately effective in exposing Alvarez's lie, and the government could publicly denounce anyone's false claim. Justice Kennedy said, citing the classic First Amendment opinion of Louis Brandeis,[10] the "remedy for speech that is false is speech that is true." That is, under our free speech system, rather than suppression or punishment, the remedy for bad speech is "more speech." Finally, Kennedy found there were "less restrictive means"—less restrictive than criminal punishment—to serve the government's goals. The government could construct a real-time database, showing who the actual medal recipients are, that anyone could check. The Stolen Valor Act was unconstitutional.

Kennedy got only four votes for his opinion. He needed the concurrence of Justice Breyer, joined by Justice Kagan, to make his 6–3 majority. The concurring justices agreed the law could not stand. But they thought, consistent with their position in other cases involving content-based restrictions, strict scrutiny was strong medicine, too binary, and should be sparingly used. Here, "intermediate scrutiny" was enough to condemn the law. Breyer and Kagan were concerned, among other things, that blessing this law would allow government to make lying in elections a crime (government would have a compelling interest in preventing voter deception) and that would open a real can of worms: politicians could be prosecuted for lying about their credentials or their opponents' experience, and government could choose to prosecute only those candidates it disfavored. There are lots of lies to choose from in the Trump era, but we depend on opponents and the press, rather than the criminal law, to expose them.

Justice Alito dissented. As in his dissents in the funeral protest and animal cruelty cases and his opinion in the video games case, he seemed morally offended by the notion the court would grant free speech protection for Alvarez's lie. He recalled asking Alvarez's lawyer at oral argument what truthful speech the act would "chill," and the answer was "None." In Alito's view, joined by Justices Scalia and Thomas, the act was narrowly targeted at deliberate lies about facts within the speaker's personal knowledge; the law was viewpoint neutral; and there was no risk that valuable speech would be suppressed.

This was another case in which the justices' usual voting lineup was scrambled. Kennedy, whose opinion was full of First Amendment platitudes (e.g., "Our constitutional tradition stands against the idea that we need Oceania's Ministry of Truth," citing George Orwell's *1984*), was joined by Chief Justice Roberts and two liberals, and bitterly opposed by the three hardest-core conservatives.

So, is there a "constitutional right to lie?" That does not sound like a principle that citizens could get behind and say we live in a wonderful country. But it is the wrong question. The real question concerns the extent of government power over what we say about ourselves. If what we say harms no one, no one believes our falsehood, we get no benefit from it, and it does not interfere with any societal goal, harmless fibbing is none of the government's business.

Alvarez joins the funeral-protest and animal-cruelty cases in protecting speech that has no inherent value and that the majority of citizens finds offensive. The speech did not promote the search for truth in the marketplace of ideas. Its protection was not essential to self-government. Nor was it needed to protect individual autonomy and self-fulfillment. Rather, the apparent thread connecting these decisions is that government should not be trusted to decide what speech is valuable and what is not, and this justifies limitations on the reach of government's power over what we can say.

Tea Party T-Shirts: *Minnesota Voters Alliance v. Mansky*

In the fourth in the quartet of First Amendment decisions handed down by the Roberts Court in June 2018 (along with *Cakeshop, Janus,* and *NIFLA,* discussed in chapters 2 and 3), finishing up the first century of free speech decisions, a carelessly drafted century-old law led to a Tea Party victory in the Supreme Court. The Minnesota state legislature, trying to avoid unseemly electioneering and commotion in polling places, enacted a kind of polling place dress code. It prohibited wearing a "political badge, political button, or other political insignia" in a polling place on election day.

Other provisions of the law banned putting up signs or soliciting votes within one hundred feet of a polling place. Back in 1992, the Supreme Court upheld a Tennessee law very similar to these other provisions but did not deal with electioneering in the polling place.[11] All states have laws restricting campaigning around polling places. The laws were based on the nineteenth-century experience of aggressive partisan electioneering and the resultant chaos and voter intimidation.

Andrew Cilek, a Tea Party provocateur in Hennepin County, Minnesota, wore a Tea Party T-shirt displaying the "Don't Tread on Me" serpent and a "Please I.D. Me" button to the polls for the 2010 election. (Although there was no voter identification measure on the ballot, the button was intended to call attention to the voter ID issue arising in several states.) Cilek was confronted by an election clerk and told he could not wear the T-shirt or the button in the polling place. He was initially turned away. He was later allowed to vote, but his name and address were recorded for a potential criminal follow-up investigation.

The Minnesota Voters Alliance, affiliated with the Tea Party, filed a lawsuit along with Cilek challenging the statute. They argued that the apparel ban violated their free "speech" rights. Their apparel did not solicit votes for or against any candidate or ballot proposition. They asserted that the Tennessee case was distinguishable because it involved active electioneering, but the Minnesota law banned purely passive political speech. They argued the law was overbroad and vague, and its vagueness would allow election officials to discriminate against voters with disfavored political leanings.

The federal court of appeals upheld the law, concluding it was a viewpoint-neutral measure that advanced the state's valid interest in "peace, order, and decorum" in the polling place. There was no serious burden on political speech, since the law applied only for the few minutes a voter would be in the polling place.

This was an easy case for the Roberts Court.[12] Chief Justice Roberts wrote the opinion for the 7–2 majority. He acknowledged the state had a valid interest in providing a calm environment in which voters could carry out their solemn civic duty of casting their votes. He recounted the history of crude electioneering that gave rise to laws like those in Minnesota and Tennessee. He acknowledged that a polling place is not a traditional public forum like a sidewalk or park, a place where one might expect to hear disputatious or partisan speech. States are free to decide that "some forms of advocacy should be excluded from the polling place." Roberts also noted that the Minnesota law was not viewpoint based; it treated all political views equally; it banned "political" clothing or insignia regardless of party, persuasion, or point of view. In these circumstances, the court applied forgiving scrutiny, requiring only that the speech restriction be "reasonable."

The problem with the Minnesota law was the inability to identify, with any precision, what was prohibited. The term "political" was not defined, and the justices found it impossible to discern clear lines so that the law could be consistently applied. At the oral argument, they peppered the state's lawyer with hypothetical questions (e.g., whether the law prohibits caps or shirts saying "Make America Great Again," "National Rifle Association," "ACLU," "AARP," or "All Lives Matter"; quoting the text of the Second Amendment or the First Amendment; or depicting a rainbow flag), and did not get satisfactory answers. Although there was no evidence of improper or partisan abuse by election clerks, imprecise laws invite inconsistent or biased discretionary enforcement. Chief Justice Roberts concluded the Minnesota law was not "capable of reasoned application."

Justices Sotomayor and Breyer, in dissent, thought the court should have given Minnesota a chance to construe the law in a way that would provide reasonable certainty about its meaning, and they would have referred the question to the state's supreme court.

*　　*　　*

The court seems to be more protective of politicking in polling places than in a venue much closer to home: the marble plaza in front of the Supreme Court building. A federal law bans any kind of demonstration or display of signs and banners on the court grounds. Court officers have admonished protestors who have ventured onto the plaza, and they arrested one man standing quietly with a sign complaining of police misconduct against minority groups. The District of Columbia Court of Appeals upheld the law, and in 2016, the Roberts Court declined to hear the case.[13] Back in 1983, the court had held the statute unconstitutional as applied to the sidewalks in front of the courthouse.[14] But the Roberts Court was unwilling to consider the challenge in its own front yard. Can a citizen wear a Tea Party T-shirt on the plaza? In the courtroom?

While the result in the Minnesota case benefitted a politically conservative organization, there is no evidence the decision was ideologically motivated. Let's hope the outcome would have been the same if the challengers had been Peace and Freedom or Green Party members.

Trademarks and Hate Speech: *Matal v. Tam*

When Simon Tam started his Asian-American rock band, he could not have anticipated a trip to the US Supreme Court for a milestone case with his name on it denying there is a "hate speech" exception to the First Amendment. Nor would he have expected supplying another occasion for the Roberts Court to use the First Amendment to limit government regulation of business.

Tam named the band the Slants. He knew "slants" was a racial slur, a derogatory term for persons of Asian descent. The idea was to use, publicize, and thereby "reclaim" the term and "take ownership" of stereotypes about people of Asian ethnicity. The band played, toured, and recorded under its name. Two of the band's albums were *The Yellow Album* and *Slanted Eyes, Slanted Hearts.*

Tam applied to the US Patent and Trademark Office for a trademark on the name. The office denied the application, based on a federal law prohibiting the registration of trademarks that may "disparage . . . persons, living or dead." The examining official determined that "a substantial composite of persons [would] find the term in the applied-for mark offensive." Tam took the case to federal court, and the court of appeals held the "disparagement" clause of the law unconstitutional. Next stop, Supreme Court.

In the Roberts Court, the government argued that trademarks are "government speech," not private speech and therefore not subject to the First Amendment at all.[15] Government must speak on all kinds of subjects and, when it does, it is not subject to First Amendment restraints. It can engage in viewpoint discrimination. For example, government can put up posters that support a war effort and a conscription drive, but government is not required to put up posters that encourage resistance to the draft. When it regulates private speech, it cannot discriminate by viewpoint; but when it speaks, it does not have to be viewpoint neutral.

The court unanimously rejected the government's position and affirmed the judgment for Tam. Justice Samuel Alito wrote the court's opinion. Though he himself had authored an important precedent on the government speech issue (the one mentioned in chapter 4 allowing a city to keep its Ten Commandments monument in a public park),[16] he warned that the "government speech" doctrine is "susceptible to dangerous misuse." If "private speech could be passed off as government speech by simply affixing a governmental seal of approval, government could silence or muffle the expression of disfavored viewpoints." If trademarks are government speech, what about copyrights? Could the government deny copyright to a book because it disparages someone?

It was "far-fetched" to say a trademark is government speech, Alito said. "The Federal Government does not dream up these marks, and it does not edit marks submitted for registration." If trademarks were government speech, the federal government would be "babbling prodigiously and incoherently." The government would be "unashamedly endorsing a vast array of commercial products and services," mouthing slogans such as "Just do it" (Nike) and "Have it your way" (Burger King). Allowing federal registration of a mark does not convert private speech into government speech.

The government also argued that Tam was free to *use* the name the "Slants," and no one was stopping him from engaging in any other speech. Denying the trademark merely denied the benefits of registration, such as easier enforceability. This was a kind of government subsidy program. But the vice of the disparagement provision was that it discriminated on the basis of viewpoint, allowing praise of certain groups but not disparagement. Justice Alito:

> To be sure, the clause evenhandedly prohibits disparagement of all groups. It applies equally to marks that damn Democrats and Republicans, capitalists and socialists, and those arrayed on both sides of every possible issue. It denies registration to any mark that is offensive to a substantial percentage of the members of any group. But in the sense relevant here, that is viewpoint discrimination: Giving offense is a viewpoint.

The provision therefore violated the First Amendment.

Justice Alito wound up his opinion with a major pronouncement on hate speech. He noted that the government claimed an interest in "preventing 'underrepresented groups' from being 'bombarded with demeaning messages in commercial advertising.'" The government said it had an interest in "preventing speech expressing ideas that offend." An *amicus curiae* brief by Native American Organizations concerned about trademarks like the "Washington Redskins" supported the government's effort to encourage "racial tolerance" by denying a trademark. But Justice Alito bluntly said, "That idea strikes at the heart of the First Amendment. Speech that demeans on the basis of race, ethnicity, gender, religion, age, disability, or any other similar ground is hateful; but the proudest boast of our free speech jurisprudence is that we protect the freedom to express 'the thought that we hate.'" (These are surprising words from Justice Alito, the sole dissenter in the funeral protest hate speech case.)

Justice Alito's list of the kinds of persons who may be demeaned is typical of various "hate speech" regulations. The *Tam* decision (together with the funeral-protest decision) could not be a clearer rejection of attempts to ban "hate speech."

The court's ruling can be viewed—properly—as still another win for both "commercial speech" (that's what trademarks are) and for the business interest in avoiding government regulation. The court was saying businesses are entitled to brand and market their products and services any way they wish (so long as they do not confuse consumers or infringe others' property rights). Justice Alito found a serious

> problem with the argument that commercial speech may be cleansed of any expression likely to cause offense. The commercial market is well stocked with merchandise that disparages prominent figures and groups, and the line between commercial and non-commercial speech is not always clear, as this case illustrates. If affixing the commercial label permits the suppression of any speech that may lead to political or social 'volatility,' free speech would be endangered.[17]

Tam was clearly a victory for business interests.

Two years after *Tam*, the court confronted a different provision of the trademark law, one banning registration of marks
that are "immoral" or "scandalous." Eric Brunetti applied for a
"FUCT" trademark for his clothing line, that the trademark office denied. The court found this provision unconstitutional as
viewpoint discrimination.[18] As in *Tam*, "a law disfavoring 'ideas
that offend' discriminates based on viewpoint." Writing for the
court, Justice Kagan also noted that the provision "results in
viewpoint discriminatory *application*," pointing to inconsistent
trademark grants and denials where the government favored
or disfavored certain viewpoints. All justices agreed that the
"immoral" provision was invalid. Fearful the marketplace will
be flooded with offensive trademarks, four justices said a narrower "scandalous" provision—one aimed only at marks that
are "obscene, vulgar or profane"—would be valid.

Sex Offenders on Social Media:
Packingham v. North Carolina

On the same day as *Tam*, the court decided its first social media
First Amendment case.[19] Lester Packingham was a twenty-one-
year-old college student when he had sex with a thirteen-year-
old girl. He pleaded guilty to taking indecent liberties with a
child and served his time. He was required by North Carolina law to register as a sex offender. Eight years later, a state
court dismissed a traffic ticket against him. He logged on to
Facebook and posted this: "Man, God is Good! How about I
got so much favor they dismissed the ticket before court even
started? No fine, no court cost, no nothing . . . Praise be to
GOD, WOW! Thanks JESUS!"

North Carolina law made it a felony for a registered sex
offender "to access a commercial social networking Web site
where the sex offender knows that the site permits minor children to become members or to create or maintain personal

Web pages." (Oddly, the law exempted sites devoted to photo-sharing, email, instant messaging, or chat rooms—sites that might appeal to both children and predators.)

A police officer discovered that Packingham had accessed Facebook. The state did not allege that he had contacted a minor or committed any other illicit act on the Internet. But Packingham was convicted and given a suspended prison sentence.

The Roberts Court unanimously reversed Packingham's conviction, finding the state law unconstitutional. Justice Kennedy's majority opinion launched into an over-the-top encomium of social media and "the Cyber Age [as] a revolution of historic proportions." He said cyberspace has "vast potential to alter how we think, express ourselves and define who we want to be." Noting that this case is "one of the first this Court has taken to address the relationship between the First Amendment and the modern Internet," Justice Kennedy said, "the Court must exercise extreme caution" before limiting access to the Internet. He likened the Internet to streets and parks as a "quintessential forum" for the exchange of views and information.

However, the North Carolina law seemed to be content neutral: it was a restriction on access to the Internet, not a restriction on what can be said. Therefore, the law was not subject to strict scrutiny. Justice Kennedy applied "intermediate scrutiny," requiring the law to be "narrowly tailored to serve a significant governmental interest" and not to "burden substantially more speech than is necessary to further the government's legitimate interests."

Justice Kennedy concluded that

the statute here enacts a prohibition unprecedented in the scope of First Amendment speech it burdens. . . . North Carolina with one broad stroke bars access to what for many are the principal sources for knowing current events, checking ads for employment, speaking and listening in the modern public square, and otherwise exploring the vast realms of human thought and knowledge.

In other words, the ham-handed law burdened more speech than necessary to serve the state's purpose of keeping convicted sex offenders away from vulnerable victims.

Concurring, Justice Alito, joined by the chief justice and Justice Thomas, had no doubt the law barred offenders from a "vast array of websites, including many that appear to provide no realistic opportunity for communications that could facilitate the abuse of children." The statute "sweeps far too broadly to satisfy the demands of the Free Speech Clause." But Alito said Justice Kennedy's "loose rhetoric" itself swept far too broadly. Objecting to Justice Kennedy's "equat[ing] the entirety of the internet with public streets and parks," Justice Alito said Kennedy's "undisciplined dicta" belied his call for proceeding with Internet cases "circumspectly, taking one step at a time."

In an odd way, the *Packingham* ruling recalls the "better things" the First Amendment used to protect. There was no obvious corporate or Christian right interest at stake in the case (notwithstanding Packingham's thanks to Jesus). Rather, the case involved a lone former convict who wanted to use a free medium to express his feelings about his experience in a court case—and was criminally punished for wholly innocent speech. That's the kind of libertarian case in which the First Amendment should play its proper role.

The Roberts Court's libertarian rulings are not inconsistent with its rulings favoring business and the religious right. Indeed, as noted, some of them have directly favored business and fundamentalist religious interests. Moreover, the First Amendment principles invoked in the libertarian cases are readily available for use as deregulatory weapons.

CONCLUSION

Time to Reconsider
First Amendment Principles?

Justice Kagan was right. The politically conservative justices on the Roberts Court have been systematically weaponizing the First Amendment in ways that serve the interests of business and the Christian right, invalidating democratically enacted laws and threatening routine business regulations.

This development coincides with the discovery by right-wing demagogues of the political value of demanding greater free speech. Starting with his campaign and carrying over into his presidency, Donald Trump and his ideological comrades—the Milo Yiannopoulises and Ann Coulters of the world—have shifted the First Amendment conversation. Instead of dissidents and the dispossessed, it is these conservative ideologues who are clamoring for "free speech" at public universities and elsewhere, sneering at "political correctness" and ridiculing attempts to curb "hate speech."[1]

The Roberts Court's weaponization of the amendment should give pause to those who reflexively say it is always good when the court rules in favor of free speech. The *Lochner* era, when the court aided and abetted the excesses of the Industrial Revolution by interpreting the Fourteenth Amendment to block social welfare laws and economic regulations, was not good for America. As Justice Breyer wrote in a book on constitutional interpretation, "No one wants to replay that discredited history in modern *First Amendment* guise."[2] Retired Justice

John Paul Stevens wrote in a recent book that *Lochner* was the prime example of "improper judicial activism."[3] Chief Justice Roberts himself warned against "reviv[ing] the grave errors of that period."[4]

It is worth recalling Justice Holmes's dissent in *Lochner v. New York*,[5] criticizing the justices' reliance on "an economic theory which a large part of the country does not entertain," and reminding us that the "constitution is not intended to embody a particular economic theory." After all, the words "free enterprise," "capitalism," and "corporation," do not appear anywhere in the Constitution; there is no reason they should be singled out as deserving of special constitutional stature. Nor, as Holmes cautioned, should a small band of unelected judges be picking and choosing, based on their preferred economic theory, who wins and who loses on the issues of the day.

The Roberts Court has been accomplishing *Lochner*ian goals by substituting the First Amendment for the Fourteenth. It has been doing this in several ways:

- It has stretched "speech" beyond recognition to spare businesses from inconvenient regulation, as it did for the pharmaceutical industry in *Sorrell* (holding that buying and selling drug prescription data was protected speech);[6] to weaken public employee unions as in *Janus* (treating an obligation to pay for services rendered as "compelled speech");[7] to further antiabortion efforts as in *NIFLA* (relieving antiabortion clinics from the obligation to post notices about their services and state-provided services); and to empower corporations and wealthy individuals, as in *Citizens United* (treating "independent expenditures" as protected political speech incapable of creating corruption or its appearance).

- It has overruled longstanding, well-established precedents to reach its desired results, as in *Citizens United* and *Janus*.

• It has been blurring the distinction between "commercial speech" (e.g., advertising and required corporate disclosures) and public discourse and the distinction between corporate speech and individual citizen speech.

• It has applied First Amendment principles inconsistently, leaving them in disarray and allowing the justices to emphasize whatever principles lead to their desired result.

• It has—through its virtually invisible selection process, under which it has complete discretion to hear or reject a petition—managed its docket to engineer politically conservative outcomes.

*   *   *

There is no quick fix, but fair, open-minded, and impartial justices, endowed with life tenure, should take a fresh look at the court's First Amendment jurisprudence, with particular attention to the following points.

"Abridging the freedom of speech"

These few words in the First Amendment raise three different questions in every case: Is what the speaker wants to say or do "speech"? Is the proposed speech within "the freedom" of speech? Is the government restriction "abridging" the freedom of speech?

First, the court should reexamine what will be deemed "speech." The Roberts Court's commodious definition of speech is unmoored from the reasons why we protect speech. To merit recognition, the speech should relate to the purposes for according constitutional protection: Does it help us ascertain the truth in the marketplace of ideas? Does it assist democratic self-government? Does it promote individual autonomy and self-fulfillment? The only reason to grant constitutional protection for commercial speech is when it provides useful information to consumers and the public, so the court should be reluctant to erase the distinction between commercial speech and public discourse. "Speech" is not a monolithic concept. Different kinds of speech should get different First Amendment consideration.

Second, every First Amendment case to reach the court implicitly requires the court to determine whether the speech in question comes within "the freedom" of speech. The amendment does not say "no law . . . abridging speech." It recognizes, as the court has always recognized, that whatever can be called speech is not absolutely protected. Accordingly, in every case the justices must decide whether the particular speech should come within the freedom. What are the contours and limits of that freedom? Again, this determination should be made in light of the purposes of according constitutional protection to speech. Justices should be alert to situations in which, in Justice Kagan's words, there is a "realistic possibility that official suppression of ideas is afoot," situations in which a law discriminates "on the basis of viewpoint" or "restricts 'discussion of an entire topic.'"[8] Not every conceivably content-based restriction should be held unconstitutional.

Third, the court needs to give some attention and content to the word "abridging." What is the government doing about the speech in question? Banning it outright and criminally punishing the speaker? That certainly constitutes abridgment. Favoring one viewpoint on an issue of public importance? Abridgment. Requiring businesses to disclose information such as food and drug warnings, earnings for an IPO, or instances of toxic contamination? Not abridgment. The court has paid no attention to this key word in the amendment. It should.

The court should rein in its new, aggressive "compelled speech" doctrine. The doctrine was first developed in the 1940s to protect Jehovah's Witnesses' students against being required to recite the Pledge of Allegiance to the American flag in violation of their religious beliefs.[9] The rationale was that "If there is any fixed star in our constitutional constellation, it is that no official, high or petty, can prescribe what shall be orthodox in politics, nationalism, religion, or other matters of opinion, or force citizens to confess by word or act their faith therein." The doctrine was applied again to excuse Jehovah's Witnesses from having to display on their license plates political slogans they disagreed with.[10] It was never applied in business regulation cases.

Now the Roberts Court has rediscovered the doctrine. It applied it with a vengeance in *Janus* and *NIFLA*. The court's development of the doctrine threatens all kinds of regulations requiring businesses to provide warnings and make disclosures. The doctrine has also become the darling of the religious right and its campaign to establish religious exemptions from anti-discrimination laws and government mandates, as in the *Masterpiece Cakeshop* case and its copycats. The doctrine should be dialed back to its origins, protecting individuals from being compelled to express political views they disagree with.

More generally, the court should reject efforts to invoke the First Amendment to achieve goals extraneous to the purposes for which we protect speech.

What Neutral Principles Should Guide the Analysis of Free Speech Controversies?

There is disagreement among the justices about the level of scrutiny they should apply to speech restrictions and—regardless of whether the scrutiny is "strict," "heightened," "exacting," "intermediate," or something else—about how to decide whether a restriction is "narrowly tailored" to serve a particular government interest.

The justices virtually never dispute the government's claim of a valid interest. They virtually always give the government the benefit of the doubt. That may be appropriate in business regulation cases. But the justices ought to be more skeptical and demanding in individual speech cases, making sure the government in fact has an important and well-defined stake and not just taking its word for it.

The main focus in most cases is on the narrow tailoring analysis. And it is here that the court's reasoning zigzags, varying from case to case and justice to justice. Justices also have conflicting views on when speech restrictions are deemed content based and strict scrutiny should be exercised.

Doctrinal incoherence and inconsistency allow the justices to pick and choose the analysis most conducive to the result they want to reach. The court ought to reexamine in a principled way the analytical framework it uses to decide free speech cases.

* * *

What are the chances the justices will retool their First Amendment jurisprudence along these lines? Slim. But not nonexistent. It is unrealistic to expect the current justices to jettison their background, training, personal philosophy, and track record. But sometimes justices do change their minds. Chief Justice Earl Warren and Justices Harry Blackmun, Stevens, and Souter —all Republicans—moved ever leftward during their tenure and ended up regarded as liberals. Justices can grow in the job.

Chief Justice Roberts in particular seems to be motivated by concern about his legacy. After all, the court will forever bear his name. His vote with the four liberals to save the Affordable Care Act can only be seen as a desire not to have the court perceived as governed by the Republican party line: hostility to anything proposed by President Obama. Roberts's new role as the court's swing vote, after the retirement of Justice Kennedy, will increase the need to be perceived as open minded and impartial. His unsolicited rebuke in November 2018 to Donald Trump's complaint that an "Obama judge" had ruled against him—"We do not have Obama judges or Trump judges, Bush judges or Clinton judges. What we have is an extraordinary group of dedicated judges doing their level best to do equal right to those appearing before them. That independent judiciary is something we should all be thankful for."[11]—was a sign of his insistence on preserving judicial independence and the presumption of impartiality. Roberts clearly does not want his court to go down in history as having subserviently carried out the political agenda of a particular party.

Nor would the other conservative justices want history to regard them as ideologues or, worse, political hacks whose votes on First Amendment issues involving certain speakers and issues were entirely predictable and who could be counted on to conform their opinions to the agenda of the Federalist Society, the Chamber of Commerce, and the Christian right.

The court should concentrate its First Amendment energy not on finding ways to liberate business from regulation but on paying attention to the "better things" the amendment was meant for. It should stay its heavy First Amendment hand regarding democratically enacted laws regulating business practices and disclosures. It should be suspicious of efforts to invoke free speech principles to serve economic and religious goals. It should endeavor to make free speech work for all, not for some, allowing the powerless as well as the powerful to have their say.

NOTES

A Personal Note

1. The case was Procunier v. Martinez, 416 U.S. 396 (1974).

2. New York Times v. Sullivan, 376 U.S. 254 (1964); and New York Times v. United States, 403 U.S. 713 (1971).

3. Abrams v. United States, 250 U.S. 616 (1919)(Holmes, J., dissenting); and Whitney v. California, 274 U.S. 357 (1927)(Brandeis, J., concurring).

4. William Bennett Turner, *Figures of Speech: First Amendment Heroes and Villains* (Oakland, CA: Berrett-Koehler, 2011); and William Bennett Turner, *Free Speech: Supreme Court Opinions from the Beginning to the Roberts Court*, rev. 1st ed. (San Diego, CA: Cognella, 2019).

5. "President Obama's Farewell Address: Full Video and Text," *New York Times*, January 10, 2017, https://www.nytimes.com/2017/01/10/us/politics/obama-farewell-address-speech.html.

6. Seth Schiesel, "Former Justice Promotes Web-Based Civics Lessons," *New York Times*, June 9, 2008, https://www.nytimes.com/2008/06/09/arts/09sand.html.

Introduction

1. Janus v. American Federation of State, County and Municipal Employees, 201 L.Ed.2d 924 (2018).

2. Rule 10, Rules of the United States Supreme Court, available at https://supremecourt.gov.

3. John C. Coates. IV, "Corporate Speech and the First Amendment: History, Data, and Implications," *Constitutional Commentary* 30, no. 2 (Summer 2015): 223, https://scholarship.law.umn.edu/con comm/546.

4. Schenck v. United States, 249 U.S. 47 (1919).

5. John G. Roberts, Jr. transcript of opening statement, at http://www.cnn.com/2005/POLITICS/09/12/roberts.statement/index.html?_s=PM:POLITICS.

6. The amendment does not say "speech" cannot be abridged. The question in every free speech case is whether the particular speech in question comes within and is thus protected by "the" freedom of speech.

7. West Virginia State Board of Education v. Barnette, 319 U.S. 624 (1943)(Frankfurter, J., dissenting).

8. Ibid.

9. Stromberg v. California, 283 U.S. 359 (1931).

10. Cohen v. California, 403 U.S. 15 (1971); and Texas v. Johnson, 491 U.S. 397 (1989).

11. Terminiello v. Chicago, 337 U.S. 1 (1949).

12. Smith v. Collin, 439 U.S. 916 (1978).

13. Shuttlesworth v. Birmingham, 394 U.S. 147 (1969).

14. New York Times v. Sullivan, 376 U.S. 254 (1964).

15. Lochner v. New York, 198 U.S. 45 (1905).

16. Testimony of John G. Roberts, Jr., Hearing on the Nomination of John G. Roberts, Jr. to be Chief Justice of the United States, September 14, 2005, 408, https://www.judiciary.senate.gov/imo/media/doc/GPO/CHRG-Roberts.pdf.

17. Obergefell v. Hodges, 192 L.Ed. 2d 609, 643 (2015) (Roberts, Ch. J., dissenting).

18. Lewis F. Powell, Jr., "An Attack on American Enterprise System" (memorandum submitted to US Chamber of Commerce, August 23, 1971) [hereafter cited as "Powell memorandum"], http://law2.wlu.

edu/deptimages/Powell%20Archives/PowellMemorandumPrinted.
pdf.

19. Zachary Roth, "How the Chamber of Commerce Conquered the
Supreme Court," MSNBC (September 13, 2013), http://www.msnbc.
com/msnbc/how-the-chamber-commerce-conquered-the-sup.

20. Obergefell v. Hodges, 192 L.Ed. 2d 609, 656-658 (2015).

21. Chief Justice Roberts attended Federalist Society meetings and
was listed in its membership directory, but at the time of his nomination, he distanced himself from the society, saying he was not and
never had been a member. Joan Biskupic, *The Chief: The Life and Turbulent Times of Chief Justice John Roberts*, 130 (New York: Basic Books,
2019).

22. The Federalist Society, "About Us," on the society's website,
https://fedsoc.org/about-us.

23. Ronald Reagan, "Ronald Reagan's First Inaugural Address,"
January 20, 1981, https://www.presidency.ucsb.edu/documents/
inaugural-address-11.

24. John Roberts in particular was "captivated" by Reaganism and
felt that Reagan was "speaking directly to me" in his inaugural address. Biskupic, *The Chief*, 64 and chapter 3. "The five years that Roberts devoted to Reagan ignited a quiet passion in him and clarified
his ideological views." Ibid. at 87.

25. The court's website contains brief, official, somewhat antiseptic
biographies of the justices, https://www.supremecourt.gov/about/
biographies.aspx.

26. National Federation of Independent Business v. Sibelius, 567
U.S. 519 (2012).

27. Lanell Williams-Yulee v. The Florida Bar, 191 L.Ed. 2d 570
(2015).

28. Belmont University College of Law, "A Conversation with
Chief Justice John Roberts" (February 2, 2019), https://news.bel
mont.edu/honorable-john-g-roberts-jr-chief-justice-of-the-united
-states-speaks-at-belmont-university/.

29. Linda Greenhouse, "Justice Clarence Thomas's Solitary Voice," *New York Times,* June 8, 2016, https://www.nytimes.com/2016/06/09/opinion/justice-clarence-thomass-solitary-voice.html.

30. Linda Greenhouse, "Is Clarence Thomas Supreme Court's Future?," *New York Times,* August 2, 2018, https://www.nytimes.com/2018/08/02/opinion/contributors/clarence-thomas-supreme-court-conservative.html.

31. McKee v. Cosby, No. 17-1542 (February 19, 2019) (Thomas, J., concurring in denial of certiorari); New York Times v. Sullivan, 376 U.S. 254 (1964).

32. Fellow originalist Neil Gorsuch testified at his confirmation hearing that *Sullivan* had been "the law of the land for, gosh, 50, 60 years." *Sullivan* had been a target of candidate Donald Trump's hope to "open up" the libel laws so he and others could "make lots of money." See Ted Johnson, "Trump's Supreme Court Nominee Cites His Decision in A&E Case in Query over Libel Laws," *Variety,* March 21, 2017, https://www.yahoo.com/entertainment/trump-supreme-court-nominee-cites-decision-e-case-210344568.html.

33. Linda Greenhouse, "It's All Right with Sam," *New York Times,* January 7, 2015, https://www.nytimes.com/2015/01/08/opinion/its-all-right-with-samuel-alito.html.

34. She was charged with contempt of Congress for failure to turn over documents on hazardous waste dumps. Philip Shabecoff, "House Charges Head of E.P.A with Contempt," *New York Times,* December 17, 1982, https://www.nytimes.com/1982/12/17/us/house-charges-head-of-epa-with-contempt.html.

35. Bush v. Gore, 538 U.S. 98 (2000).

36. CBS News, "Sotomayor Explains 'Wise Latina' Comment," July 14, 2009, https://www.cbsnews.com/news/sotomayor-explains-wise-latina-comment/.

37. Pamela S. Karlan, *Stanford Law Faculty on Justice Scalia's Legacy* (blog), Stanford Law School Stanford University, Stanford, CA, February 15, 2016, https://law.stanford.edu/2016/02/15/stanford-law-faculty-on-justice-scalia/.

38. McConnell has said that not filling the Scalia vacancy was "the most consequential thing I've ever done." See Charles Homans, "Mitch McConnell Got Everything He Wanted, *New York Times Magazine*, 35, 52, January 27, 2019, https://www.nytimes.com/2019/01/22/magazine/mcconnell-senate-trump.html.

39. Ross Douthat, "Anthony Kennedy's Imperial Legacy," *New York Times*, July 1, 2018, https://www.nytimes.com/2018/06/30/opinion/sunday/anthony-kennedys-imperial-legacy.html.

40. FCC v. Pacifica Foundation, 438 U.S. 726 (1978).

41. "On Cameras in Supreme Court, Souter says, 'Over my Dead Body,'" *New York Times*, March 30, 1996, https://www.nytimes.com/1996/03/30/us/on-cameras-in-supreme-court-souter-says-over-my-dead-body.html.

Chapter 1

1. Citizens United v. Federal Election Commission, 558 U.S. 310 (2010).

2. First National Bank of Boston v. Bellotti, 435 U.S. 765 (1978).

3. Austin v. Michigan Chamber of Commerce, 494 U.S. 652 (1990).

4. For a detailed account of the court's predecision back and forth, see Jeffrey Toobin, "Money Unlimited: How Chief Justice Roberts Orchestrated the Citizens United Decision," *New Yorker*, May 21, 2012.

5. Unless otherwise noted, all quotations in the discussion of Citizens United are from the reported opinions in that case.

6. Buckley v. Valeo, 424 U.S. 1, 19 (1976).

7. New York Times v. Sullivan, 376 U.S. 254 (1964).

8. New York Times v. United States, 403 U.S. 713 (1971).

9. Adam Liptak, "A Clue on His View of Citizens United," *New York Times*, July 24, 2018.

10. Brown v. Board of Education, 347 U.S. 483 (1954).

11. Emphasis in original; the italics are Roberts's.

12. Justice Stevens cited President Roosevelt's 1905 annual message to Congress as quoted in United States v. Automobile Workers, 352 U.S. 567, 572 (1957).

13. It does treat "the press" separately, as though the press may have different rights than those included in "the freedom of speech." Justice Stevens thought this was an indication the framers could indeed believe the amendment permitted distinctions based on the speaker's identity.

14. Santa Clara County v. Southern Pacific Railway Co., 118 U.S. 384 (1886).

15. In Roe v. Wade, 410 U.S. 113, 157 (1973), Justice Blackmun collected nine provisions referencing a "person" in the body of the Constitution and three in amendments other than the Fourteenth. All of them clearly referred to natural persons, not corporations.

16. Freund is quoted in Anthony Lewis, *Freedom for the Thought That We Hate* (Basic Books, New York 2007), 178.

17. SpeechNow.org v. FEC, 599 F. 3d 686 (D.C. Cir. 2010).

18. Federal Election Commission, Advisory Opinion 2010–11 (July 22, 2010).

19. Jan Crawford, "Alito Winces as Obama Slams Supreme Court Ruling," *CBS News*, January 28, 2010, https://www.cbsnews.com/news/alito-winces-as-obama-slams-supreme-court-ruling/.

20. American Tradition Partnership v. Bullock, 567 U.S. 516 (2012).

21. Arizona Free Enterprise Club's Freedom PAC Club v. Bennett, 564 U.S. 721 (2011).

22. McCutcheon v. Federal Election Commission, 134 S.Ct. 1434 (2014).

23. Williams-Yulee v. The Florida Bar, 191 L.Ed. 2d 570 (2015).

24. National Federation of Independent Business v. Sebelius, 567 U. S. 519 (2012).

25. City of Berkeley, November 2014 Ballot, Proposition P (November 4, 2014).

26. State of California Official Voter Information Guide, Proposition 59 (November 2016).

27. See, for example, Floyd Abrams, "Citizens United: Predictions and Reality," in *The Free Speech Century*, ed. Lee C. Bollinger and Geoffrey R. Stone (New York: Oxford University Press, 2019), 83. Abrams states that "polling data has consistently indicated that upwards of 80% of the public, on a totally bipartisan basis, disapproves of the ruling."

Chapter 2

1. Janus v. American Federation of State, County, and Municipal Employees, 201 L.Ed. 2d 924 (2018).

2. Abood v. Detroit Board of Education, 431 U.S. 209 (1977).

3. Senator Rand Paul, "Government Unions in the Crosshairs" (2017 fundraising letter, copy on file with author).

4. Knox v. Service Employees International Union, 567 U.S. 298 (2012).

5. Harris v. Quinn, 131 S.Ct. 2618 (2014).

6. Powell said, "I agree with the court as far as it goes, but I would make it more explicit that compelling a government employee to give financial support to a union in the public sector—regardless of the uses to which the union puts the contribution—impinges seriously upon interests in free speech and association protected by the First Amendment." Abood v. Detroit Board of Education, 413 U.S. 259, 255 (1977).

7. Friedrichs v. California Teachers Association, 194 L.Ed. 2d 255 (2016) ("affirmed by an equally divided court").

8. Linda Greenhouse, "A Question of Legitimacy Looms for the Supreme Court," *New York Times*, June 21, 2018, https://www.nytimes.com/2018/06/21/opinion/supreme-court-janus-unions.html.

9. William Baude and Eugene Volokh, "Compelled Subsidies and the First Amendment," *Harvard Law Review* 132, no. 1 (November 2018): 171, 204.

10. Unless otherwise noted, all quotations in this chapter are from the opinions in *Janus*.

11. Keller v. State Bar of California, 496 U.S. 1, 14 (1990).

12. Board of Regents of University of Wisconsin v. Southworth, 529 U.S. 217, 233 (2000).

13. Glickman v. Wileman Brothers & Elliot, Inc., 521 U.S. 457, 474 (1997).

14. See Baude and Volokh, "Compelled Subsidies and the First Amendment."

15. Justice Kagan was not the first to complain that "black-robed" judges were exercising illegitimate power to strike down democratically enacted laws. When the shoe was on the other foot, Justice Scalia, dissenting from the court's ruling that invalidated the Defense of Marriage Act, said the "black-robed supremacy" was seizing power it did not have. See United States v. Windsor, 133 S.Ct. 2675, 2698 (2013). Similarly, his vituperative dissent in the same-sex marriage case, Obergefell v. Hodges, 192 L.Ed. 2d 609 (2015), asserted that "A system of government that makes the People subordinate to a committee of nine unelected lawyers does not deserve to be called a democracy."

16. Uradnik v. Inter Faculty Organization, No. 18-719 (petit. for certiorari filed December 4, 2018; cert. denied April 29, 2019).

Chapter 3

1. Michael Bobelian "With Kavanaugh, Trump Could Fashion the Most Business-friendly Supreme Court since the New Deal," *Forbes*, July 10, 2018, https://www.forbes.com/sites/michaelbobelian/2018/07/10/in-nominating-kavanaugh-trump-could-fashion-the-most-business-friendly-court-since-the-new-deal/#67686a1b6fda.

2. James Surowiecki, "Courting Business," *New Yorker,* March 7, 2016. See also Adam Liptak, "Friend of the Corporation," *New York Times,* May 5, 2013.

3. Jeffrey Rosen, "Supreme Court, Inc.," *New York Times Magazine,* March 16, 2008, https://www.nytimes.com/2008/03/16/magazine/16supreme-t.html.

4. Epic Systems v. Lewis, 200 L.Ed. 2d 889 (2018).

5. AT&T Mobility LLC v. Concepcion, 563 U.S. 333 (2011).

6. American Express Co. v. Italian Colors Restaurant, 559 U.S. 1103 (2013).

7. Wal-Mart Stores, Inc. v. Dukes, 564 U.S. 338 (2011).

8. Ledbetter v. Goodyear Tire & Rubber Co., 550 U.S. 618 (2007).

9. Michigan v. EPA, 135 S.Ct. 2699 (2013).

10. Mutual Pharmaceutical Co. v. Bartlett, 133 S.Ct. 2466 (2013).

11. John C. Coates IV, "Corporate Speech and the First Amendment: History, Data, and Implications," *Constitutional Commentary* 30, no. 2 (Summer 2015): 223, https://scholarship.law.umn.edu/con comm/546/.

12. Sorrell v. IMS Health, Inc. 564 U.S. 552 (2011).

13. 564 U.S. at 557. Unless otherwise noted, all quotations in the discussion of *Sorrell* are from the court's reported opinions.

14. The italics are Justice Breyer's.

15. See, e.g., Valentine v. Chrestensen, 316 U.S. 52 (1942) (upholding ordinance forbidding distribution of leaflets with commercial advertising).

16. Virginia State Board of Pharmacy v. Virginia Citizens Consumer Council, 425 U.S. 748 (1976).

17. Coates, "Corporate Speech and the First Amendment," 223.

18. Ibid.

19. Robert Post and Amanda Shanor, "Adam Smith's First Amendment," *Harvard Law Review* 128 (March 2015): 165.

20. See, for example, Justice Thomas's concurring opinions in Matal v. Tam, 198 L.Ed. 2d 366 (2017) and in Liquormart v. Rhode Island, 517 U.S. 484, 517 (1996).

21. New York Times v. Sullivan, 376 U.S. 254 (1964).

22. McKee v. Cosby, No. 17-1542 (February 19, 2019).

23. Reed v. Town of Gilbert, 192 L.Ed. 2d 236 (2015).

24. Unless otherwise noted, all quotations from Reed are from the justices' published opinions.

25. Justice Thomas was quoting from Cincinnati v. Discovery Network, Inc., 507 U.S. 410, 429 (1993).

26. See Adam Liptak, "Court's Free-Speech Expansion Has Far-Reaching Consequences," *New York Times* (August 17, 2015), https://www.nytimes.com/2015/08/18/us/politics/courts-free-speech-expansion-has-far-reaching-consequences.html, noting that the decision can be invoked to challenge securities regulation, drug labeling, and consumer protection, among other matters.

27. Justice Kagan was quoting from R.A.V. v. St. Paul, 505 U.S. 377, 386 (1992).

Chapter 4

1. Town of Greece v. Galloway, 134 S.Ct. 1811 (2014).

2. Pleasant Grove City v. Summum, 555 U.S. 460 (2009).

3. Salazar v. Buono, 559 U.S. 700 (2010). See also American Legion v. American Humanist Ass'n, No. 17-1717 (June 20, 2019) (State may retain Latin Cross on public land).

4. Hein v. Freedom from Religion Foundation, 551 U.S. 587 (2007).

5. Arizona Christian School Tuition Organization v. Winn, 563 U.S. 125 (2011).

6. Trinity Lutheran Church v. Missouri, 198 L.Ed. 2d 551 (2017).

7. Burwell v. Hobby Lobby, 134 S.Ct. 2751 (2014).

8. Masterpiece Cakeshop v. Colorado Civil Rights Commission, 138 S.Ct. 1719 (2018).

9. The Trump Administration weighed in, filing an *amicus curiae* brief on behalf of the United States. It chose to argue that the Colorado enforcement of its antidiscrimination law violated the baker's free speech rather than his religious rights, contending that a "custom wedding cake is a form of expression." See Brief for United States, No. 16-111, filed September 7, 2017.

10. Town of Greece, 134 S.Ct.1811.

11. Had this view prevailed, Phillips could have placed a sign in his store window saying, "Wedding cakes for heterosexuals only."

12. Arlene's Flowers v. State of Washington, 201 L.Ed. 2d 1067 (2018). The court did exactly the same thing in 2019. After several months of mulling over another wedding cake case, the court summarily threw out a ruling against a different baker and sent the case back to an Oregon court for "further consideration in light of *Masterpiece Cakeshop*." Klein v. Oregon Bureau of Labor and Industries, No. 18-547 (June 17, 2019). Because the Kennedy opinion provided no guidance whatever on the free speech issue, it is hard to know what the state courts are supposed to consider. It is apparent that the justices are simply unwilling at this point to confront such a politically contentious issue.

13. McCullen v. Coakley, 134 S.Ct. 2518 (2014).

14. Unless otherwise noted, all quotations are from the justices' *McCullen* opinions.

15. Reed v. Town of Gilbert, discussed in chapter 3, which would have supported their argument, had not yet been decided.

16. National Institute of Family and Life Advocates v. Becerra, 138 S.Ct. 2361 (2018) (cited as *NIFLA*).

17. Unless otherwise noted, all quotations are from the justices' opinions in the NIFLA case.

18. Planned Parenthood v. Casey, 505 U.S. 833 (1992).

19. CTIA-The Wireless Association v. City of Berkeley, No. 17-976 (June 28, 2018), vacating 843 F.3d 774 (9th Cir. 2017) (denial of rehearing), 854 F.3d 1105 (9th Cir. 2017) (panel opinion).

20. American Beverage Association v. City and County of San Francisco, 916 F.3d 749 (9th Cir. 2019).

Chapter 5

1. Morse v. Frederick, 551 U.S. 393 (2007).

2. Tinker v. Des Moines Ind. School Dist., 393 U.S. 503 (1969).

3. Bethel School Dist. v Fraser, 478 U.S. 675 (1986).

4. Hazelwood School Dist. v. Kuhlmeier, 484 U.S. 260 (1988).

5. Morse v. Frederick, 551 U.S. at 404–405.

6. Beard v. Banks, 548 U.S. 521 (2006).

7. Jones v. North Carolina Prisoners Labor Union, 433 U.S. 119 (1977).

8. Garcetti v. Ceballos, 547 U.S. 410 (2006).

9. Civil Service Commission v Letter Carriers, 413 U.S. 548 (1973).

10. Parker v. Levy, 417 U.S. 733 (1974).

11. Rumsfeld v. Forum for Academic and Institutional Rights, 547 U.S. 47 (2006).

12. Holder v. Humanitarian Law Project, 561 U.S. 1 (2010).

13. Amanda Shanor and Robert Post, "Adam Smith's First Amendment," *Harvard Law Review* 128, no. 5 (March 2015): 165, 179.

Chapter 6

1. The Federalist Society, "About Us," https://fedsoc.org.

2. See, for example, United States v. Abrams, 250 U.S. 616 (1919) (Holmes, J., dissenting); and Whitney v. California, 274 U.S. 357 (1927) (Brandeis, J., concurring).

3. Snyder v. Phelps, 562 U.S. 443 (2011).

4. United States v. Stevens, 559 U.S. 460 (2010).

5. Miller v. California, 413 U.S. 15, 24 (1973).

6. Brown v. Entertainment Merchants Ass'n, 564 U.S. 786 (2011).

7. Ginsberg v. New York, 390 U.S. 629 (1968).

8. Federal Communications Commission v. Fox Television Stations, 556 U.S. 562 (2009).

9. United States v. Alvarez, 567 U.S. 709 (2012).

10. Whitney v. California, 274 U.S. 357 (1927).

11. Burson v. Freeman, 504 U.S. 191 (1992).

12. Minnesota Voters Alliance v. Mansky, 138 S.Ct. 1876 (2018).

13. Hodge v. Talkin, No.13-863 (May 16, 2016).

14. United States v. Grace, 461 U.S. 171 (1983).

15. Matal v. Tam, 198 L.Ed. 2d 366 (2017).

16. Pleasant Grove City v. Summum, 555 U.S. 460 (2009).

17. Justice Thomas wrote a concurring opinion in *Tam* repeating his position that restrictions on "commercial speech" must satisfy strict scrutiny.

18. Iancu v. Brunetti, No. 18-0302 (June 29, 2019).

19. Packingham v. North Carolina, 198 L.Ed. 2d 273 (2017).

Conclusion

1. On March 2, 2019, President Trump said he would sign an executive order denying federal funds for colleges and universities that do not allow conservative speakers and student organizations to speak. See Michael D. Shear, "Trump Says He Will Sign Free Speech Order for College Campuses," *New York Times,* March 2, 2019, https://www.nytimes.com/2019/03/02/us/politics/trump-free-speech-colleges.html?action=click&module=Top%20Stories&pgtype=Homepage.

2. Stephen Breyer, *Active Liberty: Interpreting our Democratic Constitution* (New York: Knopf, 2005), 41 (emphasis added).

3. John Paul Stevens, *The Making of a Justice: Reflections on My First 94 Years* (New York: Little Brown, 2019), 149.

4. Obergefell v. Hodges, 192 L.Ed.2d 609 (2015) (Roberts, Ch. J., dissenting). Roberts denounced the "unprincipled" decision making of the *Lochner* era.

5. Lochner v. New York, 198 U.S. 45, 75 (1905) (Holmes, J., dissenting).

6. *Sorrell v. IMS Health, Inc.*, discussed in chapter 3.

7. *Janus v. American Federation of State, County, and Municipal Employees,* discussed in chapter 2.

8. Reed v. Town of Gilbert, 192 L.Ed. 2d 236 (2015) (Kagan, J. , concurring). Justice Kagan quoted from Davenport v. Washington Ed. Assn., 551 U.S. 177, 189 (2007), Rosenberger v. Rector and Visitors of Univ. of Virginia, 515 U.S. 819, 829 (1995); and Consolidated Edison Co. v. Public Service Commission of New York, 447 U.S. 530, 540 (1980).

9. West Virginia State Bd. of Education v. Barnette, 319 U.S. 624 (1943).

10. Wooley v. Maynard, 430 U.S. 705 (1977).

11. Adam Liptak, "Chief Justice Defends Judicial Independence After Trump Attacks 'Obama Judge,'" *New York Times,* November 21, 2018, https://www.nytimes.com/2018/11/21/us/politics/trump-chief-justice-roberts-rebuke.html.

SUGGESTIONS FOR FURTHER READING

Books

Joan Biskupic, *The Chief: The Life and Turbulent Times of Chief Justice John Roberts* (New York: Basic Books, 2019). Straightforward biography of the chief justice.

Lee C. Bollinger and Geoffrey R. Stone, eds., *The Free Speech Century* (New York: Oxford University Press, 2019). Collection of scholarly essays on the first century of free speech decisions.

Erwin Chemerinsky and Howard Gillman, *Free Speech on Campus* (New Haven: Yale University Press, 2017). First Amendment issues arising on college campuses regarding provocative outside speakers, academic freedom, and hate speech.

Noah Feldman, *Scorpions: The Battles and Triumphs of FDR's Great Supreme Court Justices* (New York: Twelve, 2010). Intertwined biography of four great and influential Supreme Court justices appointed by President Roosevelt and their legacy.

Linda Greenhouse, *The US Supreme Court: A Very Short Introduction* (New York: Oxford University Press, 2012). Concise and readable account of how the court works, including the chief justice's role.

Thomas Healy, *The Great Dissent: How Oliver Wendell Holmes Changed his Mind—and Changed the History of Free Speech in America* (New York: Metropolitan [Henry Holt], 2013). Intellectual history of how Justice Oliver Wendell Holmes established modern free speech principles.

Anthony Lewis, *Freedom for the Thought that We Hate: A Biography of the First Amendment* (New York: Basic Books, 2007). Extended essay recounting First Amendment history and the role of free speech in American society.

Anthony Lewis, *Make No Law: The Sullivan Case and the First Amendment* (New York: Random House, 1991). Masterful history of free speech in America and the inside story of the great decision in *New York Times v. Sullivan.*

Jane Mayer, *Dark Money: The Hidden History of the Billionaires Behind the Rise of the Radical Right* (New York: Doubleday, 2016). How billionaires like the Koch brothers have bankrolled efforts to achieve conservative and libertarian goals.

David E. McCraw, *Truth in Our Times: Inside the Fight for Press Freedom in the Age of Alternative Facts* (New York: All Points Books, 2019). Lawyer for the *New York Times* recounts First Amendment adventures in the Trump era.

Burt Neuborne, *Madison's Music: On Reading the First Amendment* (New York: New Press, 2015). Provocative criticism of the Roberts Court's First Amendment jurisprudence and argument that courts should consider the amendment's full forty-five-word text and hear "Madison's music."

Robert Post, *Citizens Divided: Campaign Finance Reform and the Constitution* (Cambridge, MA: Harvard University Press, 2014). *Citizens United* and campaign finance reform, with scholarly commentary.

John Paul Stevens, *Five Chiefs: A Supreme Court Memoir* (New York: Little, Brown, 2011). The retired justice's memoir of working with five chief justices over his long career.

John Paul Stevens, *The Making of a Justice: Reflections on My First 94 Years* (New York: Little Brown, 2019). The justice's memoir of his tenure on the court.

Geoffrey R. Stone, *Perilous Times: Free Speech in Wartime from the Sedition Act of 1798 to the War on Terrorism* (New York: Norton, 2004). Comprehensive history of First Amendment and constitutional analysis in times of threats to national security.

Nadine Strossen, *Hate: Why We Should Resist It with Free Speech, Not Censorship* (Oxford: University Press, 2018). Essay and constitutional analysis on efforts to ban "hate speech."

Jeffrey Toobin, *The Oath: The Obama White House and the Supreme Court* (New York: Doubleday, 2012). Account of the early years of the Roberts Court and the conservative justices' ideological struggles during the Obama administration.

William Bennett Turner, *Figures of Speech: First Amendment Heroes and Villains* (Oakland: Berrett-Koehler, 2011). The characters and issues involved in free speech controversies, including cases handled by the author.

William Bennett Turner, *Free Speech: Supreme Court Opinions from the Beginning to the Roberts Court*, revised 1st ed. (San Diego: Cognella, 2019). Opinionated casebook with edited text of the court's decisions and commentary on the first century of free speech opinions.

Laurence Tribe and Joshua Matz, *Uncertain Justice: The Roberts Court and the Constitution* (New York: Picador [Henry Holt], 2014). The Roberts Court justices and their decisions through 2014, with a chapter on *Citizens United* and a chapter on the court's early free speech decisions.

Melvin Urofsky, *Dissent and the Supreme Court: Its Role in the Court's History and the Nation's Constitutional Dialogue* (New York: Vintage, 2017). History of great dissenting opinions and their role in changing public perceptions and the law.

Adam Winkler, *We the Corporations: How American Businesses Won their Civil Rights* (New York: Liveright [Norton], 2018). History of how business corporations acquired legal "personhood" and now exercise civil rights protecting their interests.

Useful Websites

https://www.scotusblog.com. Daily news and analysis of cases decided and pending in the court, calendars, statistics, and scholarly commentary.

https://oyez.org. Comprehensive collection of all the court's decisions through history and to date, including audio and transcripts of oral arguments.

https://supremecourt.gov. The court's website, with opinions as they are filed, justices' biographies, court rules and procedures, and searchable dockets of all briefs and documents filed in cases.

INDEX

CREDITS

ACKNOWLEDGMENTS

Thanks to:

- My students over the last three-plus decades at UC Berkeley, first in the Graduate School of Journalism and then in the Media Studies major, whose questions made me look for answers.

- My "career-free" peers who were my students in recent years at the Fromm Institute at the University of San Francisco and at the Osher Lifelong Learning Institute at UC Berkeley, whose life experiences contributed to my understanding.

- Professor Melvyn H. Zarr of the University of Maine Law School, my law school classmate, colleague at the NAACP Legal Defense Fund, gifted teacher, and friend, whom I inveigled into reading drafts of chapters and whose suggestions I shamelessly incorporated.

- The amazing Molly Turner, who in between teaching, recording and launching a series of podcasts, and consulting on technology and the cities, found time to critique big parts of the book—way beyond the call of daughterly duty.

- Deirdre Greene and Nigel Quinney of Roaring Forties Press, who saw this book as worth publishing and then effortlessly made it happen.

ABOUT THE AUTHOR

For thirty-three years, William Bennett Turner has taught courses on freedom of speech and the press at the University of California, Berkeley.

He practiced law for forty-five years, doing constitutional and civil rights litigation. He argued three cases before the US Supreme Court (including two First Amendment cases) and many more cases in federal appellate courts and state supreme courts, and he served as lead counsel in many notable state and federal trials.

After graduating from Harvard Law School, Turner had a Fulbright fellowship in comparative law and then spent three years with a New York law firm and ten years with

the NAACP Legal Defense Fund. He returned to teach at Harvard in 1977, and then he founded his own law firm in San Francisco.

His previous books are *Free Speech: Supreme Court Opinions from the Beginning to the Roberts Court* (Cognella 2019) and *Figures of Speech: First Amendment Heroes and Villains* (Berrett-Koehler 2011).

CPSIA information can be obtained
at www.ICGtesting.com
Printed in the USA
FSHW021506111119
63973FS